When I first started going into th   d,
I know why you want me to go in there. You want   x
those men." God said, "No Rog, I'm sending you in there to
fix you!" So very true Lord.

—Pastor Roger
Pastors to Prisoners

"What Satan intended for evil, God can use for good. These
powerful stories are proof that the Lord is in the business
of restoring broken lives."

—Chad LaComb
Fully Restored Ministries

"And the Lord added to the church daily those who were
being saved." Acts 2:47b. I consider myself so very blessed
and fortunate to have been called to prison ministry. It has
built up my faith and trust in Jesus like nothing I could ever
imagine. People ask me all the time, "Randy, what is prison
ministry like?" My own words fail. The best description I
can give is that it is very much like the Book of Acts. As
one fellow servant says, "I see miracles every time I go."
Whether you might be called to prison ministry or not, I
know these true testimonies by beloved brothers will build
you up, touch your soul and make you cry. I firmly believe
that Jesus is preparing soldiers on the inside for the coming
revival outside.

—Randy Cocking
Inside Out Prison Ministry

*Continue to remember those in prison as if you were
together with them in prison, and those who are mistreated
as if you yourselves were suffering. Hebrews 13:3*

100% of all proceeds from this book will go back into purchasing copies to send into correctional facilities and juvenile detention centers around the world. This book is for ministry and not for profit. If you know of a facility that needs a copy, please email us at planbtestimonies@gmail.com and we'll send one to the chaplain for their library. Thank you for helping us spread the message that all things are possible through Christ who strengthens us!

Cover artwork by Jay McCurry - now on the "outside."
Thank you, Brother, for sharing your beautiful gift with us!

"PLAN B"

When Your Plan Fails and God's Prevails.

"Now have come the salvation and the power and the kingdom of our God, and the authority of His Christ. For the accuser of our brothers has been thrown down, he who accuses them day and night before our God. They have conquered him by the blood of the Lamb and by the word of their testimony; and they did not love their lives so as to shy away from death."

—Revelation 12:10-11

Dedication

First and foremost, this book is dedicated to my Lord and Savior, Jesus Christ. I walk in gratitude for my salvation every day, and I pray these testimonies will bring Him all the glory, honor and praise He deserves!

To all my brothers in blue who have stirred up my heart with their friendship and testimonies. Without you, this book wouldn't be possible. Thank you for sharing your stories in hopes that others might be inspired and hearts might be changed because of God's goodness in your lives! You always make us feel so welcome when we come to worship with you. You truly are a blessing!

To my son, Nate, who encourages me to visit and share the Gospel with those in prison. I love you, and I'm so proud to be your Mom.

And finally, to all those I serve with on the inside, our hearts are connected in a way that I cannot explain. There is just something about those who long to go where most won't. We know the true blessing and love that overflow from the inside, and we are the ones that are truly blessed!

Table of Contents

"Some wish to live within the sound of a chapel bell; I wish to run a rescue mission within a yard of hell."

— C.T. Studd

Acknowledgments

From Pastor Roger...

I cannot express enough thanks to Chaplain Bill Brown, the Protestant Chaplain at Richard J. Donovan Correctional Facility (aka RJ Donovan or RJD). It is his love for the Lord, his compassion for the lost men behind the wall, and his unwavering and tireless commitment to the job of chaplain that cultivated an atmosphere at Donovan for the volunteers to come in and present the various programs which reach out to the men at Donovan State Prison. Chaplain Bill, our heartfelt gratitude to you and your wife, Mary Brown, for the many years of service, from which we have all benefited.

I would like to say thank you to a man whose shoulders we all stand on here at Donovan. Pastor John "Jack" Oien is the founder and past president of *Pastors to Prisoners*. It is because of his vision and persistence that Pastors to Prisoners was founded. He laid the groundwork for what is now known as the "Yard Pastor." He has volunteered at Donovan for well over twenty years, serving and ministering to the men at Donovan. We all owe a great deal of gratitude for the great work this great man of God has done in teaching, preaching, counseling, and making disciples. Many have been won to the Kingdom because of the sacrifice that he has made, and continues to make, as the Yard Pastor on the D Yard.

When I was introduced to prison ministry back in the year 2000, I had no idea of the impact that it would have on my life. Words can't adequately express the profound love and gratitude I have experienced from the men that I have had the pleasure of serving as a volunteer at Donovan State Prison. I thank God for placing this calling on my life. I never imagined that serving in a maximum security prison would be so fulfilling and life changing. And finally, to my caring, loving, and supportive wife, Peggy (know affectionately as "Momma Peggy" to our boys in blue), my deepest gratitude. Your encouragement when times get rough is much appreciated and duly noted. To serve Christ with you by my side has been, and is, one of the greatest blessings of my life. Your love and heart for these dear brothers is truly an inspiration to me. I would also like to thank all of the amazing volunteers who co-labor with us each and every week. Who give of their time and resources and with heartfelt dedication share the love of Christ with our brothers behind the wall.

I would like to thank Warden Daniel Paramo and Community Resource Manager, Robert Brown, for their leadership and support, for without their guidance and approval, none of this would be possible.

From Jenn....

For all the brothers whose testimony didn't make it in here, they'll live in our hearts and encourage us as we continue to serve behind the walls! Keep the faith, and thank you for your faithfulness.

Pastor Roger and Peggy Ziegler - your teaching and love for the brothers, not just at R.J. Donovan, but in all the prisons you visit, is inspiring. Thank you!

My Pastor, Mike Reed, and my church, Calvary Chapel Oceanside, for having a heart for evangelism.

My team, *Inside Out of Prison Ministry*, whose love for those in prison shines so brightly that anyone who comes in contact with them is going to be impacted by their testimonies. You made me WANT to go in and meet these amazing brothers and sisters. And Sheri, well, what would I do without you sister? I love you!

To my friends, Chad, Vernon and Tamara - honestly, your testimonies and love for others has radically changed my life.

To my counselor, Judy, and Pure Life Ministries, thank you for loving me enough to take a hardened heart and soften it by using the Word of God to teach, rebuke, correct and train me in righteousness. I am a new creation because of it!

To my pen pal and friend, Mark Carney, who became a brother from inside the walls while I was growing up - you're now with the Lord, but your friendship will never be forgotten!

To my mom who prayed for me to get my life right with Christ in high school and showed me how to love the lost by taking me to Wayside Honor Rancho as a teen to visit the incarcerated.

And finally to my sisters in Christ, Chris and Siobhan, thank you for editing this book of love! I appreciate your time and devotion to something I'm so passionate about!

" God uses men who are weak and feeble enough to lean on him. "

— Hudson Taylor, Missionary to China

Introduction

In this book you will hear about a wonderful prison ministry program called "Kairos." If you would like more information about it, you can go to their web site at www.kairosprisonministry.org.

The Gospel of Jesus Christ is alive and well behind prison walls and while some might believe prison is the end of the road for men and women who have gone astray, those of us who volunteer on the inside see how it can be a brand new beginning for them. I've heard many say that before they came to Christ they felt unloved, discarded by society, lost, confused and without purpose. Yet, when they are introduced to Jesus, their hearts became filled with meaning, acceptance, faith, hope and the greatest of these, which is love. They discovered a new family right where they're at. They found that the church isn't a building, but a body of believers who can come together and embrace them for who they are, as they are. I, too, have found my place among them. I am at home when I'm in their presence. For those who are in Christ Jesus there is no condemnation. We are all one in Spirit, and it's such a privilege to serve, worship and grow in my walk with the Lord, right along side them. They have brought healing to my heart, a purpose to my step, and for that I am so very thankful.

I thank my God every time I remember you. In all my prayers for all of you, I always pray with joy because of your partnership in the gospel from the first day until now, being confident of this, that he who began a good work in you will carry it on to completion until the day of Christ Jesus.

It is right for me to feel this way about all of you, since I have you in my heart and, whether I am in chains or defending and confirming the gospel, all of you share in God's grace with me. God can testify how I long for all of you with the affection of Christ Jesus.

And this is my prayer: that your love may abound more and more in knowledge and depth of insight, so that you may be able to discern what is best and may be pure and blameless for the day of Christ, filled with the fruit of righteousness that comes through Jesus Christ—to the glory and praise of God. Philippians 1:3-11

Love You All,
Sister Jenn

Dear Brother,

Hello, my name is Nate and I wanted to write to you and tell you that you are loved. My dad left us when I was 9 and was put in jail for the rest of his life. I hope you can find the same peace and restoration that I have as God fills the hole that my dad never did. As a quote from a book (called The Father You've Always Wanted by Ed Tandy McGlasso sais "No matter what kind of father you had or didn't have — You can have the father you've always wanted"). I highly reccomend this book, it explains how even when you feal the heavyness of not having a dad, God can lift you up and make you Whole again.

love,

Nate, 13

A 13-year-old Boy Named Nate

My name is Ryan. I'm 33 years old and am currently serving a sentence of life without the possibility of parole at R. J. Donovan Correctional Facility. This is my testimony of how Jesus Christ saved my life from further destruction.

I grew up in Long Beach, California. No brothers, no sisters, no father, just Mom and me. I grew up extremely poor and around lots of drugs, gangs and violence.

At the young age of seven years old, I was placed in juvenile hall for six months. I was ADHD and had a lot of pain and hurt inside that I held onto all throughout my life. As a result of that anger and pain, I got into a lot of trouble. As I got older, people would try to tell me about God, and I vowed I would have no part of it. I would usually respond with profanity and get angry with them.

By the time I hit twenty-one years of age, I was arrested and convicted for murder during a robbery gone bad, involving drugs. I blamed God for everything. I cursed God. I hated God for allowing me to grow up in such poverty and for allowing me to grow up without a father. I blamed Him for all the abuse I experienced as a child and now for my life sentence.

As I got to prison, I became involved in prison gangs, drugs and more violence. The violent culture in prison only made me worse and made me hate God more. I couldn't believe how such a loving, caring, forgiving God would allow me to experience such pain and hurt in my life. Satan had really distorted my mind so bad that I began to worship other gods and attend "Odinist" services. Attending "Odinist" services only made me more angry and hateful, as their teachings are to persecute Christians.

As I began to fall into this deep, dark, lonely, hopeless pit that I created, I began to contemplate suicide. I was ready to end it all and be done with life on earth. To make matters worse, several days before Kairos, the prison guards conducted a cell search of my cell and confiscated all my personal property. I had come to the conclusion that suicide was my only answer. I hit rock bottom and couldn't take it anymore.

I was told about Kairos, and that I would be placed down as an alternate, but God had other plans. A fellow buddy of mine was supposed to attend but subsequently was placed in Ad Seg "the Hole!" He was a professed Odinist member whose teachings are against Christianity.

I figured I'd go ahead and go, to get the heck out of my cell, because my cell mate was driving me crazy, plus I knew all about the cookies. Little did I know, God had a serious awakening and plan for me that I didn't know about.

> "Deep down inside something was changing. I didn't feel out of place. I felt such a peace around me."

As I began to attend Kairos on the first day, I felt awkward and out of place. I remember thinking, "I'm not coming back tomorrow." As the second day came and my cell door opened, my cell mate said, "Are you going bro?" I said, "Yeah bro, I'm going, they've got coffee." As I began to walk over there to the chapel, I had to put on my smiley face and pretend I was in a good mood. Upon entering the room, I sensed such a completely different atmosphere. Deep down inside something was changing. I didn't feel out of place. I felt such a peace around me. Later on that day I went with all the Kairos members to eat, and upon returning, I was given a letter addressed to me. It was from a 13-year-old boy named Nate.

In that letter, Nate told me how his dad left when he was nine years old and was put in jail for the rest of his life. Nate told me how God gives him peace and restoration and how God fills that hole in his heart that his Dad never did. Nate told me how God, and only God, can be the Father I always wanted and can lift me up and make me whole again. At that very moment I burst into tears and felt such a peace and restoration come over me. I knew at that very moment that I was foolish all these years and blinded by Satan for not believing God. God used Nate to reach me and to soften my heart. For years I was blinded by Satan. I lived in the dark; I turned to other gods. Since coming to know Christ, I have found peace, joy, happiness, hope and love.

Looking back at my life, worshiping other gods, I can now say it felt like God was saying, "Son, you wouldn't listen to my commandments, you continued sinning, you turned to drugs, but I won't have you worshiping other "gods." God had enough of my defiant ways, and He knew it was time for change. God has begun such an awesome transformation in my life. In an instant, God changed my heart and way of thinking. I know for certainty that He loves me. He disciplines those He loves. God has shown me His love, compassion and mercy. He's rescued me from suicide, drugs and a hopeless life. My hope is in Jesus Christ, my Lord and Savior. My life is no longer in chaos and madness. I wake up with such joy and peace now and hope in Jesus Christ's return.

God truly saved my life. I know God loves me so much that He sent his only Son to die for our sins while we were still sinners. God is merciful to forgive if we repent and turn away from sins. I pray that my story will help those who hear it to understand how much of a loving, caring, understanding God He is. He's merciful and forgiving. If God can change the heart of me—a drug addict, robbing, lying, cheating, addictive murderer—He can change anyone.

God is real and alive today, waiting for you to call upon Him and repent. I pray that the world will come to know Jesus Christ, and that they find healing, love, peace, and restoration, as I have in my almighty Father, the One, and ONLY true living God!

"For I know the plans I have for you, declares the Lord, plans to prosper you and not to harm you, plans to give you hope and a future."

Jeremiah 29:11

Have You Seen Jesus Lately?

"I was naked and you clothed Me, I was sick and you visited ME, I was in prison and you came to Me." Matthew 25:36-40

"And the King will answer and say to them, "Assuredly, I say to you, inasmuch as you did it to one of the least of these my brethren, you did it to me."

> *My fate, according to the world, had been sealed, however, Jesus had something else in mind. I just didn't know it*

I simply write these two powerful scriptures to tear away the veil that so many, today, find themselves hiding behind. It's very easy to show up to church on Sundays, or even volunteer at one of the more "comfortable" missionary outreaches, but when it comes to the stigma of going into a prison, fear, amongst many other worrisome thoughts, comes into play, not to mention that of judgment of what some might deem as the "dregs" of society, who are a menace to society. However, Jesus stated boldly in Matthew that those who went into prison, indeed, visited Him. Then there are those who were at Jesus' left whom were rebuked with an eternal judgment, simply put, "depart from Me, you cursed into everlasting fire." If there was ever something to be fearful of, it would be that of Christ's eternal judgment.

My name is Kevin, and I've been in prison for twenty-four years. For the first thirteen, I was lost, completely engulfed in sin, with no cares or concerns of a brighter future or hope thereafter. I killed a man who preyed upon and molested me at a young age. I grew up in a stable home, yet I was lost and totally selfish. I had gone to church with my parents; yet, for me, it was for all the nefarious reasons, and by the time I reached nineteen, I found myself on the way to Folsom State Penitentiary. My fate, according to the world, had been sealed; however, Jesus had something else in mind. I just didn't know it.

My addiction to drugs increased. I harbored a lot of pain and resentments and had no clue as to how to deal with them. Alone, I sought acceptance from those around me. No sooner did I find that acceptance than I rose through the ranks of becoming a bona fide prison gang member. I was a validated skinhead, a title that my family would surely be ashamed of; yet, I hid behind it as a twisted badge of honor.

Becoming so lost in the demented world, I soon found myself locked away in the famed Pelican Bay Segregated Housing Unit, or as we on the inside call it, the Special Housing Unit (S.H.U.). I was given a sentence of "indeterminate," meaning that I would never again see past the concrete cubicle and razor wire that surrounded me. I was deemed a threat to the safety and security of the institution. You're probably thinking by now that I deserved it, or that I made my bed and now must lie in it. But let me remind you, that's not what Jesus had in store. Locked away in seclusion, watching one year fade into the next, there didn't seem a reason to live for. After all, I was serving a life sentence and was sure to die alone in prison.

Out of the blue one night, I received a letter from a distant cousin, whom I hadn't heard from in decades. She began sharing with me the gospel of Jesus Christ, all of which I wanted nothing to do with. Yet, she persisted, and like the truth of the Word, it pierced the marrow of my soul, breaking the tough exterior of a skinhead. In 2004, I found myself drawn to my knees in that little concrete cubicle, alone, asking Jesus to forgive me of my sins and to come into my life. There's been no looking back since.

All the restrictions that society and prison had placed on me soon began to crumble. My indeterminate stint in Pelican Bay was no more. I began sharing the Word with other hardened nmate souls, and with prison officials, seeing their lives changed for eternity. I continued this ministry until 2011, when I was transferred to R. J. Donovan Correctional Facility n sunny San Diego.

This is where my new identity in Christ was nourished. Brothers and sisters in Christ, filled with hearts of love for God and love for the brethren, were evident from the very start. I was being challenged and edified, and in turn, was edifying those coming in from the outside. It was all about Jesus and continues to be that to this day.

There is a dire passion for many who come into this place, and that passion is for Jesus Christ. After all, Jesus came to save the outcasts of the world, too, and to heal the sick, in need of the Great Physician. I share this because of the joy it is to see Jesus truly at work in the place—the impact of transformed lives, miraculous healings and a liberty that some never could have imagined.

In 2014, I was granted parole, and it's all to the glory of my Lord and Savior, Jesus Christ, alone. Being a new creation has proven evident, and if it wasn't for the love, prayers and devotion of my dear brothers and sisters in Christ, I could have easily still been locked away with no hope of any sort.

I encourage you—come visit Jesus in prison. After all, obedience is better than sacrifice. You will truly be changed and blessed, eternally, being assured that unfading crown of glory.

May the love and peace of Jesus continue to manifest in your lives!

Your fellow servant in Christ Jesus,
Kevin

" Their work will be shown for what it is, because the Day will bring it to light. It will be revealed with fire, and the fire will test the quality of each person's work. "

1 Corinthians 3:13

Trial by Fire

Part I – Ezekiel 34:16

I was seventeen years old when I was sentenced to prison, matching the years of my life and capping the wasted years of my youth on the streets.

My trial by fire could not have begun at a more appropriate place than the worst and most violent level-IV prison in California. There is no way to describe the constant mental and physical violence of the place. My life had been reduced to that of a gladiator awaiting the door to open and begin fighting for my life, at the expense of another.

The years went by quickly, leaving just a blur and too many skeletons to haunt whatever life remained in me. My heart was broken and held together by anger and hate. And then they let me out of prison.

I had nowhere else to go, so I returned to my mother's house. With all the strength I possessed, I held on to the dream of finally going "home" where there would be no more sorrow, hurt, and the pain would finally cease. However, there were forces already chipping away at my dream. Upon my release, my family was not there to pick me up and take me home. I made it home on my own, and the welcome I received was one of genuine surprise and sort of guarded. My mom's roommate was there to give me the heads-up on what was going on. He was selling drugs and storing stolen property in the house! My first night at home was spent on the couch, because they had a couple in my room. In reality, they did not believe I would be coming home. The second night at home, I lay in bed surrounded in darkness so complete that not even a trace of light was visible. When it reached inside of me I no longer had control. I began to cry, which quickly turned to sobbing that left my entire body exhausted and weak. This was something I had never experienced or allowed to be a part of my life. But with a primal rush it overwhelmed me and left me feeling completely alone. Obviously, the dream I was holding on to was quickly becoming a nightmare home. There was no home and never would be for me!

Everything I had fought for and believed to be true was a lie, a cruel joke. No one cared or ever would care. In spite of being out of prison, I now found myself in a different, stronger prison, and I truly felt I could never leave or escape.

Eventually, I found some peace in a woman, who would later become my wife (now ex-wife), but she could not deal with all the baggage I brought to the relationship. Besides, it wasn't fair to expect anyone to deal with the broken man I was.

When things became rough and we struggled for everything, drugs, and the crime to obtain them, became my only priority. My wife became second class, and the only thing that mattered or brought me comfort or peace was the drugs. My new prison now had me in chains.

It did not take long for me to get re-arrested and sent back to prison. I was so lost and hurt inside that I wanted to go back to prison. I was convinced this is where I belonged. I was meant to fight and be fed in a cage. I served nothing but a life of pain, suffering, violence and the scars to prove it was not a dream. I willfully surrendered my life to the bars that held me and vowed to never fight to better myself. Little did I know that everything I was going through was for a reason, and although it was not clear at the time, there was a purpose.

Part II, Romans 8:28-29
Upon my return, I arrived at the Northern Reception Center (DVI). I met and became a close friend, and like a brother, with my cellie, William. Eventually I was transferred to R. J. Donovan Correctional Facility. We stayed in touch through his parents, a tie that reached the point of being adopted into their family. They treated me with love and genuine care, something altogether new to me. They worried about

ny health and future plans. It began to soften my heart and unbeknown to me, God began His work in me.

> " *Their love of God prioritized my pain and heartache. I would later learn it was the heart of a Christian.* "

Around the same time, my wife and I decided to get a divorce. It crushed me. Just when I felt a little hope, it vanished! That's when God placed a couple of Christians in my path to watch over me. One I knew for a long time, and he wouldn't let me out of his sight; he refused to let my anger and pain defeat me. Another's quiet love listened to and shouldered my tears and helped me from the ground to my knees.

If not for these two angels I would have let go, or worse. I began to think I wouldn't be missed and this world would be better off without me. Fortunately for me, God had put the right people in my life at the proper moment, as I listened to and embraced my pain. My heart softened a little more, and it was then that these angels asked me to attend Kairos 100. Because of their kindness I agreed to go.

Part III, 1 Corinthians 13
During Kairos, the barriers surrounding my heart began to fall. The simple and incredible act of love administered by entire Christian families—men, women and even children— overwhelmed me. One man's love of Christ tore down the last wall inside of me. His faith and love allowed the Lord to bring us together. Truly, I now understood the death and glorious resurrection of Jesus Christ! It was no longer a fairy tale, but a gift from God through His Son, to finally free me from sin and death. It was then I truly saw the face of Jesus, as He made His home in my heart.

However, I was suddenly hit with a wave of panic. I realized my idea of love, and how love was, was totally wrong! I was afraid I could not love God in the right way. It may sound silly, but it was something serious. So I wrote my concerns down on a piece of paper and literally slipped it to the Kairos brother I mentioned earlier: "If I have never known the love of a father or mother, how do I know how to love?"

> " If I have never known the love of a father or mother, how do I know how to love? "

I will never forget the tears in his eyes as he wrote back and told me about God's incredible love, and while we were still rebellious and dead to sin, He gave His only Son for us (John 3:16). I still keep that note in my Bible. After that exchange, I went to him and we talked. Towards the end of our conversation he asked me to pray for him, because he had recently filed for bankruptcy and was in jeopardy of losing everything. I asked him why he was at Kairos for four days and not at work? He simply replied, "I'm here for you." This gift I received was, without question, from a Father who pours out His love onto his children. At this point I thought it could not get any better, but God was just getting warmed up.

Part IV, 2 John 1:6
"Deny yourself, pick up your cross and follow me."
God made me his child, He's given me love so abundantly, answered each of my prayers, and now, I cannot even deny his presence in my life!

He's both nurtured and taught me how to live my life in the manner he intended—to be like his son, Jesus, who changed my life in a dramatic way. I no longer depend on drugs or rely on anger to resolve conflicts, and the prison that's confined me for too long is gone. God has taken me as I was and created a "new" me, filling me with the happiness of his love and forgiveness. So I've taken up my cross and follow Jesus Christ, every day. I live for the opportunity, the awesome blessing, to share his promise with someone who is where I was.
And still there are doubters. I was once asked, "Where are the miracles now?" I simply responded, "I once sought the

darkness, because I was afraid to see what and who I had become, and God has shown me the radiance of his forgiving light, and that I was a child of Christ. The miracle was and is displayed in his love. I am loved—loved by a Father who created me, knew me before all creation, and knew me as I was formed in the womb. He will never forsake me. He'll protect and provide me with everything I'll ever need. I have stopped trying to control everything in my life, as I surrender my life to His will."

This wonderful miracle of life, which I now share, is not something we can do for ourselves. It is something God does in us, providing we allow Him to. At the same time, what He does in and for us is not just for our benefit, rather for everyone seeking comfort and a place at our Lord's Table. My duty is as clear as the Lord's light, allow it to shine with Him, in us and through us, and share the gospel of His love with everyone (Mt. 28:19).

My name is Jay, a believer of Jesus Christ and a willing servant of the Father... Son... Holy Spirit.

"The Lord is near to all who call on him, to all who call on him in truth. He fulfills the desires of those who fear him; he hears their cry and saves them."

Psalm 145:18-19

I Thought Death Was My Only Refuge

Greetings to you in the glorious name of our Lord and Savior, Jesus Christ. I am a servant of Christ, even though I am doing life in prison. It is my joy to share with you a brief part of my testimony of when the Lord opened my eyes to the truth.

I was on the verge of committing suicide by killing as many correctional officers as I could before being taken out. The darkness that had invaded my mind, heart and soul was so powerful that I was convinced that death was my only refuge. I was so deeply tormented by guilt, shame and loneliness that I believed that there was no hope, and I just wanted it all to end, until the day when a very odd, but happy encounter occurred.

> **God's love began to break through the darkness of my heart.**

Unknown to me, someone had put my name in for Kairos, and I was selected. The Kairos weekend just happened to be a few days before I planned to go on my rampage. I decided it could wait until after Kairos. On the first day of Kairos, I remember telling all of the volunteers, "All I want are your cookies, not your religion." For the first three days, I listened to all of the talks from the outside team. I tried to be patient and kind, as they demonstrated God's love in action, not just words. On the third day of Kairos, I was given a gift of unimaginable worth. It wasn't money or food, but it was what I needed more than anything. It went much deeper than the physical; it went straight to the heart.

I was given a letter of encouragement. God's love began to break through the darkness of my heart. The light of His love was almost too much to bear. His glorious light illuminated my dark, murderous heart. The next morning around 2:30 am, I couldn't sleep, so I read and ate some more cookies. I stopped and cried out to God, "If you are real, show me a miracle." Nothing happened. Again, I shouted, "If you are God, then let me know it, show me a miracle." It was then when God spoke to my heart. He said, "Son, you are reading your miracle." It was true. Since my Mom died three years before, I had not received one single letter. My mom was the only person who ever wrote me.

I cried out to the Lord early that morning, while in my cell, and He saved me. But I want you to think about this—where would I be today if you hadn't taken the time to write that letter? It's been almost three years since I've given my life to Christ. I have never been so happy and content. Even though I am doing a life sentence, I have seen God use me in this place to bring others to the saving knowledge of Christ. I no longer want to die. I want to live, and I want to serve Jesus with my whole heart. Thank you volunteers who come into this place regularly to bring the hope of God's love to us. You remind us that there are brothers and sisters in Christ who care about us. You bring the love that most of us never knew.

God bless you,
Brian

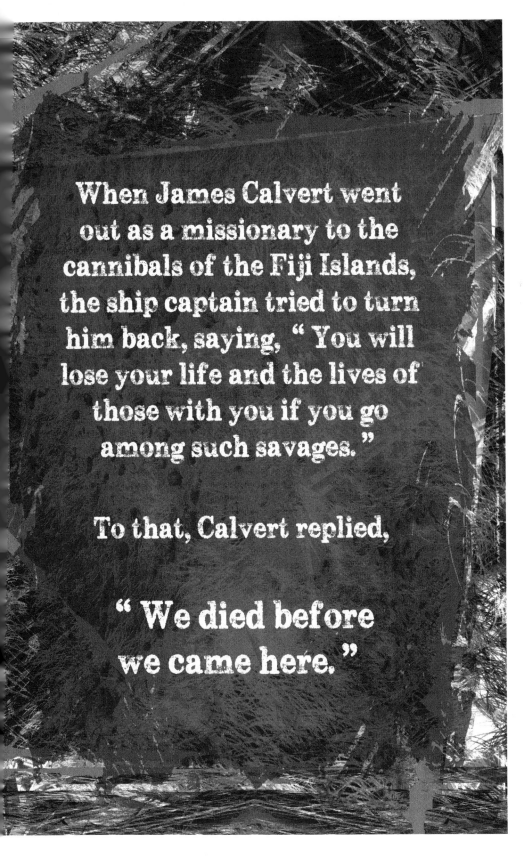

When James Calvert went out as a missionary to the cannibals of the Fiji Islands, the ship captain tried to turn him back, saying, " You will lose your life and the lives of those with you if you go among such savages."

To that, Calvert replied,

" We died before we came here."

" **And now these three remain: faith, hope and love. But the greatest of these is love.** "

1 Corinthians 13:13

Only Love

came to Kairos looking for a certificate to show the parole board. For years, I watched as men from the outside came into the yard, and men from the inside put on colorful rainbow aprons. I watched as they went into the chapel together, and I heard that cookies were consumed. Soon, they all emerged wearing leather name badges, some of them colorfully decorated. I thought Kairos was an arts and crafts class. I later learned that Kairos was a prison ministry program, but I wasn't interested. God was something "out there" and Jesus was a character for a story. Religion was a mystery, and I had no interest in reliving a childhood experience in which I had been converted into I-don't-know-what. But I was assured that Kairos would be fun and that I wouldn't be forced to do anything I didn't want to. And, I did need that certificate. So, I went in with an open mind and a willingness to receive whatever enlightenment I might find.

> "It was like the doors in my mind flew open, the lights came on, and I heard the Hallelujah chorus! Jesus is real."

What I found, however, was a group of men whose sole purpose seemed to be to make me feel welcome, comfortable and loved. I was leery of "the catch," but I saw none. ONLY LOVE. There were no strings attached, no ulterior motives, no fakers, and no requests for money or membership to an organization. ONLY LOVE. No one poked me with a bible or tried to convert me into anything. There were no lectures about fire and brimstone, no questions about my past, and no judgments about who I was. ONLY LOVE. These men just wanted to be my friend—to listen to what I had to say, to make sure I was having a good time. And whenever I was feeling a little overwhelmed, or tired, or maybe like I didn't belong, someone was right there with a smile, or a comforting hand on my shoulder, or a cookie. I watched intently at the men who came in from the outside and wondered at their spirit. I soon began to relax, to open up, and to have fun. I laughed, I sang, I danced, and I hugged. I wore a funny party hat and drew posters. I read loving notes and listened to inspiring talks and testimonials. Some made me laugh, and some made me cry. But the other men were crying, too, and that made it OK. My heart became filled with so much love, there wasn't room for anything else. So much love that it overwhelmed me and, at times, took my breath away. So much love that nothing else mattered anymore. So much love that it became a real, tangible thing. I could feel it, I could touch it, it occupied space and time. It was alive!

> **"I have a solid foundation and a joy I have never known before."**

It was right about then that someone got up and said, "Brothers, the love that you're feeling in this place, this weekend, isn't our love, it's Jesus'." I was floored. It was like the doors in my mind flew open, the lights came on, and I heard the Hallelujah Chorus! Jesus is real.

So, I came to Kairos looking for a certificate to show the parole board, and I left with Jesus in my heart and a smile on my face. Since then, I have totally immersed myself in prayer, bible study, and fellowship with my Christian Brothers. My sister and I haven't communicated in years, but when I wrote her about my Kairos experience, she wrote back and said that by coming to the Lord I had answered her prayers. She is coming to visit me next month.

Jesus has been working wonders in my life. I have a solid foundation and a joy I have never known before. I don't know what the Lord has planned for me, but I know it will be for my good and His glory. Praise God!

Kent

" Though you have not seen him, you love him; and even though you do not see him now, you believe in him and are filled with an inexpressible and glorious joy, for you are receiving the end result of your faith, the salvation of your souls. "

1 Peter 1:8-9

" He is no fool who gives up what he cannot keep to gain that which he cannot lose. "

— Jim Elliot
Missionary martyr who
lost his life in the late 1950's trying to
reach the Auca Indians of Ecuador

Numbness Started to Take Over Me

was born Jesse James, and my Pop was a tough man to please. He guided and influenced me into the boy and man I'd become. With my name being Jesse James, it was either going to be a short or a long haul. By the time I was eighteen, I was in and out of correctional facilities for almost eight years. I thought I had what it took to make it on the outside in the free world. I paroled, I entered programs, I worked 10-hour days, but I didn't have God in my life at the time. Then it happened. One argument gone wrong and I found myself back inside the walls doing a 16-year term. The journey from 2002-2014 was a nightmare. I can't even explain the loneliness, the fears, the hatred, the envy, the pride, the ego and the hell, which was everyday life behind bars.

One day in September of 2014, an altercation occurred, which I surprisingly chose to walk away from. If you asked me today why I did, I couldn't tell you. I would have normally engaged and gotten myself in trouble. But I had become numb from all the years of incarceration. The losses, the struggles and the acknowledgment that I didn't just do this to myself, but to everyone in my family—my daughter, my son, my mother, my siblings and anyone else that had any kind of love for me. I had walked away from them. I didn't think about them before—how the consequences of my actions would affect them. I never thought about my nieces and nephews that would be born while I was doing time. I wasn't able to get to get to know them from the inside, and this numbness just started to take over me.

But this is when God reached out to me through my brother, Doc. He invited me to chapel, and I felt like a dark shadow for the first time; but, the more I came, the more I trusted, and the more the darkness went away. The brighter my life became. I started to ask God to allow me to understand Him more, to long for Him more. As I prayed this prayer I began to grow in my faith.

> **"*I was going to be a free man soon. But actually, God had already freed me inside the walls.*"**

In October 2014, R. J. Donovan had a Kairos event, and I was chosen to attend. I sat and listened to all that God had to say during those three days. He used everyday men and women, like you and me, sharing their testimonies and reading facts and truths of God's grace and mercy. For the first time, I truly knew without a doubt that God existed. I knew that He had always been a part of me. I knew that Jesus Christ was my personal Savior, and I began to long more for Him and for His Word. God started to bless me and allowed a sentence reduction. Instead of doing sixteen years, I only had to serve fourteen. I was going to be a free man soon. But actually, God had already freed me inside the walls. I remember feeling sick the day before, thinking about all the "what if's," but all the volunteers in chapel encouraged me. They were honest about the struggles I would face but reminded me that greater is He that is in me, than He that is in the world. On Jan. 11, 2016, I walked out the doors of Donovan, and I'm here to say that I have become an active member at my church. I attend on Sundays, I go to the men's group, I work with my pastor on projects, like painting high schools, etc., and they have become like family to me.

God has also blessed me with an amazing fiancée, a beautiful baby boy, a home and a car. I know that each and every day, it is because I am surrounded by His grace. Don't get me wrong, every day is a struggle. It's hard out here. The struggles are real, but as long as you keep God first, He will guide you through every trial. The devil is always throwing distractions in my path, but I have walked away from all that, because I've given it to God now. My ego isn't there anymore. I'm so happy and grateful for God's amazing grace in my life!

Blessed to be alive,
Jesse James

The light shines in the darkness, and the darkness has not overcome it.
John 1:5

" The Spirit of the Lord is on me, because he has anointed me to proclaim good news to the poor. He has sent me to proclaim freedom for the prisoners and recovery of sight for the blind, to set the oppressed free... "

Luke 4:18

" No one has the right to hear the gospel twice, while there remains someone who has not heard it once. "

— Oswald J. Smith

Everyone Has a Story

Everyone has a story in here. I cannot openly share my testimony for various reasons; however, I want to. And, that s why I am writing it for you.

To start, allow me to briefly tell you about me. I am forty-two years old and grew up in So-Cal. The son of a deputy sheriff, I wanted to follow in his footsteps. I joined the Police Explorers at fourteen years old and was hired as a correctional deputy at eighteen. At nineteen, I was married and had a son and a stepdaughter before I was twenty. After about five years, I switched paths for a moment, by working in tribal government. I worked for a tribal police and later a gaming commission. This lasted a few years before I went to work as a 9-1-1 dispatcher, while attending the Police Academy. Upon graduating, I worked as a police officer, school resource officer and investigator.

> **I still didn't have God in my life. Instead, I blamed Him.**

During this time, I put the job first and did not have God in my life. In 2001, my Mother was murdered by my sister's new boyfriend of a few months. He was convicted in 2006, and is on "A Yard." I still didn't have God in my life. Instead, I blamed Him. I had a bad marriage from the gate with infidelity on both sides. I was determined to remain a family until the kids were on their own. By the end of 2005, my wife was doing things unacceptable, like taking week-long trips to Hawaii and Vegas. A little investigating on my part found she was involved with a former LAPD Rampart Cop. I again tried to reconcile our marriage, now of seventeen years. This was to no avail. I moved out, staying at friends' houses. I filed for divorce a few days before I found I had a malignant tumor in my wrist, requiring two surgeries within a week—the latter leaving me hospitalized for more than a week, alone, at Cedars-Sinai Hospital in L.A. It was during this time, I knew we were for sure finished. Despite all my trials, I was excelling at my career. Assigned as an investigator in charge of all city juvenile investigations under the Chief of Police, I was sent to a six-month course on juvenile delinquency at USC. The City got me an apartment in Marino Del Rey—walking distance to the ocean. I began dating a woman who I quickly fell in love with. I accepted that I could move forward and be happy, still with no God in my life. Three months after filing for divorce, my life was devastated. After returning to USC from having stitches removed from my wrist, I was met by an LAPD Swat Team, arrested, and taken to the District Attorney's office.

"What's changed? I walk with the Lord, pray more, fellowship, listen for His directions and try to put others before me."

I was accused of the unthinkable—molesting my step-daughter. I remember that I laughed and called my wife a bad name. I explained the recent divorce and how two days prior I had words with her on the phone, after midnight, over the kids. She told me, "Your career is over. I will ruin your world." Nothing changed, and in fact, it got worse. I had an attorney, but I sat in jail over two years, while the D.A. stacked trumped-up charges against me. My father told me, "Son, now you need to start reading the Bible." And I did. My trial lasted three months. My 16-year-old son testified, as did his girlfriend, and many friends and family. But that didn't help me with the D.A.'s "loaded case" against me. She told the jury, "I will make an example out of him. He is a disgrace to the badge." My attorney said she had no case and no evidence of the accusations. Anyone in the law enforcement field knows in a case like this you don't need evidence. In the end, I was sentenced to 134 years to life for something I didn't do. I lost everything I'd worked so hard for. Oh, I still have lots of support from family and friends. But I'm in prison for life.

What's changed? I walk with the Lord, pray more, fellowship, listen for His directions and try to put others before me. My faith is very strong now, and I know He has better for me than this.

In July of 2008, I was picked up by the Feds to testify against two supervisors. That took three years but was strategically used for His purpose. See, I was housed in San Bernardino, where my grandma lived. She visited me twice a week there until she passed away, June of 2011, after difficulties resulting from surgery. During this time, I got Grandma writing to me scriptures every week. I got her a Bible from the chaplain, which was her first.

Thank you for allowing me to share this with you and also helping me with my walk with God. You and the volunteers are so greatly appreciated, in Jesus' Name.

Brother D

"Have I not commanded you? Be strong and courageous. Do not be frightened, and do not be dismayed, for the Lord your God is with you wherever you go."

Joshua 1:9

Wasted Time, Now with Jesus Christ

My name is David. I'm forty-two years old and have been incarcerated for over two decades now. All the bad choices I have made in my youth have led me here. Before I tell you about my past life, I would like to tell you why I am writing this letter. I would very much like to help those young kids who are on the same track as I was, at their age. That one-way track is what led me to prison, pain and suffering. This is a life I would not wish upon anyone.

> "For the first time in a very long time, I was thinking of someone other than myself."

As of right now, I still have a life sentence, but it is just a matter of time before I get a date. Knowing this I just can't sit back and do nothing. This is why I want to work with at-risk youth; and with Jesus Christ in my life, I know He will help guide me to do so.

I was once a little boy that was abandoned by my father and then eventually by my family. This happening to me had me think and feel that I was unloved and not cared for. I felt it was only right that, if no one was going to care for me, then I shouldn't care for anyone else but myself. Feeling and thinking this way gave me the opportunity to do whatever I wanted, whenever I wanted. That, right there, caused a lot of drama for me early on. I was kicked out of almost every school I had been in, for violence. I started taking out all my problems and anger on everyone, never realizing the path I was heading on. This fueled my desire to commit crimes, mainly stealing. As I saw what path I was going down, someone who had "been there and done that" tried to talk some sense into me. He told me, "At a young age, I got involved in the street life, drinking, doing drugs, getting into trouble and not caring about the consequences. If I had someone like me to talk me out of such a life, I don't think I would have ended up where I am today."

Sadly, I didn't have anyone but me; thus, my crimes grew into something more. I ended up taking someone's life. In doing so, I took him away from his family and hurt so many people in the process, including my own family. At this time in my life, I didn't even realize it, because I was so self-centered. I was convicted of 2nd degree murder and sentenced to sixteen-to-life.

> **" I did a lot of bad things in my life; now it's my time to give back to the Lord and society. "**

I arrived at Calipatria State Prison in 1992. I was a twenty-year-old, scared, young kid. I used my fear and insecurity issues to continue down the path of destruction. I wanted to earn a name for myself. This was the start of my prison life, being housed on the level 4 yards and ending up in the S.H.U. (Security Housing Unit), still trying to find acceptance. I arrived to New Folsom in 1994 and joined a gang. I became a skinhead. I did this mostly for protection from other races and gangs and to finally be welcomed into people's lives. So now I was no longer committing crime for myself, I was doing it for others. When I was in Salinas Valley State Prison, I received a phone call saying that my daughter was going to be put up in a group home if I did not sign over custody to my aunt; so, in hopes to save her from such a place, I did. Soon after, my daughter came back into my life, after not seeing her for about thirteen years. I remember when I saw her, I went out to court, and I was behind glass and all shackled up, feeling this ache of not being able to be there for her the way I should have. She had asked me, "Dad, when are you going to get out?" WOW! That hurt me so much, because I didn't have an answer for her. I really never thought about getting out, because life meant LIFE!

Now, after many years and a lot of self-improvement, God will give me an opportunity to get out soon. However, I know I can never get the time I wasted back. Take a second and think about that. I returned from court and learned that the saying is true, "What goes around, comes around." I was assaulted. I transferred, still confused, and not knowing what to do. Finally, I decided it was time to lock up and leave the gang politics behind. I know if I had stayed on the main line, I would have never had a chance to get out of prison. I had to try for my daughter. For the first time in a very long time, someone in my life mattered to me more than I do! Shortly after, my little sister passed away of cancer. Six months later, my mother joined her while sleeping. This was devastating to me. I was losing everyone. I was so lost and pointed the finger of blame at God. Then one day in 2010, I was invited to a Kairos weekend retreat by a friend and Pastor Roger, the C-Facility Pastor. Kairos changed my life and gave me a whole new perspective on life. Once I accepted Jesus Christ as my personal savior, everything changed. Since then, God has been opening doors for me with blessings. He has given me deep peace, something I thought I would never achieve. Pastor Roger has been there for me in so many ways, and I am so thankful for that. God has my back now. I believe God is going to use me in a mighty way to bring those lost souls to salvation, like He did for me. He wants me to help others.

> *I hope I can encourage that young kid to dust themselves off and get up and do the right things in life.*

So, I will start with at-risk youth, because this is where my life took a turn for the worse. I did a lot of bad things in my life; now it is my time to give back to the Lord and society. I made a promise to myself that I will help wherever I am needed. I don't want to sit back and let C.D.C.R. take away another young life. I was that kid over two decades ago. I hope I can encourage that young kid to dust himself off and get up and do the right things in life.

I would very much like to help the next generation of kids to not become criminals. Pray for me to accomplish this. On

"Don't let the excitement of youth cause you to forget your Creator. Honor him in your youth before you grow old . . . "

Ecclesiastes 12:1

I've Been Changed

My family gave me every opportunity any child could want. I was raised going to church. My mother and grandparents had me in Sunday School every weekend. I even sang in the junior choir. But I felt something was missing. At the age of twelve, to fit in and be accepted, I started smoking weed. Shortly after that, church was a thing in my past. Although I would go on Easter, Christmas or Mother's Day, I would only go to appease my family. My name is Bradley.

By the time I was thirteen years old, I would leave school on a Friday and not come home until Sunday night. It didn't matter what it did to my home life. I was accepted by my so-called friends, the "homies." My mother would drive around looking for me in some of the worst parts of Pomona. I would hide and laugh as she asked the homies, "Have you seen my son?" Even hearing the worry and concern in her voice did nothing to move me. I was with the homies, putting in work, which means committing crimes at all cost.

My grandmother made me promise to finish school and not to drop out. So, I completed twelve years and even went into the Army to try and get my life straight. After receiving an honorable discharge for serving my country, it was right back to hanging with the homies, going to different states, selling drugs, and having all-out crime sprees on the way home. But the same things that make you laugh will make you cry. I was arrested and given three different life sentences.

Since being locked up, I have had more problems than I could have ever dreamed of. I was constantly in Ad-Seg or the S.H.U. for committing violence on others—even having my jaw broken in three places during a cell fight. That was one time that I ended up on the short side. A few years later, I spent twenty-four days in Mercy Hospital in Bakersfield with a lacerated left lung.

I have lost almost everything that I have ever loved. My grandparents, mother, one brother and many other family members. And those so-called "friends," the homies, turned their backs on me long ago. Someone once told me I would not change "until I was sick and tired of being sick and tired." It took me until I had been in prison eighteen years before I realized I was sick and tired of being sick and tired. Then I called on the Name of God.

I struggled with the changes God was making in my life, and after twenty-three years of being bounced around from prison to prison, I was sent to R. J. Donovan Correctional Facility, here in San Diego. A pastor there, Roger Ziegler, signed me up for church services, and it was so different for me. There were five to ten volunteers every week coming to share the love of God!

I was invited to Kairos, where, over a four-day period of time, the love of God was shared with me non-stop. My whole life changed. The walls I had built up over the years, and the mask I had worn, were all torn away. It was no longer "knowing about" God. I was having a relationship with Him, accepting Christ as my Savior. I have left behind being a part of any gang and now I serve Christ. The things I once did, I no longer do anymore, because I have been changed by the love of God!

Over the last four years, I have not missed a Sunday in church when services were available. I am part of the praise team now, a "Fisher of Men" for the kingdom of God. By the grace of God, I have also obtained my degree in ministry and continue to study towards a Bachelor's Degree, and hopefully beyond. But above all of that, I have the peace of God in my heart and salvation through Christ Jesus, my Lord and Savior.

"Oh, taste and see that the Lord is good; blessed is the man who trusts in Him!" Psalm 34:8

How Valuable You Are in the Sight of God

n your hands you hold a testimony that will reach up into your heart and open up your mind, wide enough to begin seeing how valuable we are in the sight of God.

LOVE. Does it exist? Is it real? Well, you would know that answer if you stepped into me and feel what I feel. Three years ago, I was miraculously healed from an ADVANCED stage of cancer. I was once an Olympic hopeful, but my healthy body dropped to almost nothing. After many cycles of chemo and two major surgeries, my doctors told me nothing more could be done.

> "Are you telling me, you'd rather die with cancer than to let JESUS heal you?"

At that time, I had a cell mate who was a Christian from Egypt. He tried to share CHRIST with me, but being a devout Muslim, I would have nothing to do with Christianity. My cell mate wasn't ready to give up on me, though. He wrote his mother in Egypt and forged a visiting document and sent both to his mother. She had her small congregation pray over some holy oil and took a plane trip half way across the world to deliver a healing from Jesus. Her act of faith stunned me, because not even my own family or friends had visited me, even as I lay ill.

When she arrived, she greeted me with a smile and a question, "Do you believe that GOD can heal you?" I responded with, "Yes, of course Allah can heal me!" She quickly replied with, "NO! NOT Allah, but JESUS!" I quickly stated that Jesus is not God, he is only a prophet. Then she asked, "Are you telling me, you'd rather die with cancer then to let JESUS heal you?" I remember her piercing stare, as if it was like Jesus looking at me. At that moment I felt love, and

" God often uses our deepest pain as the launching pad of our greatest calling."

—Unknown

Lost and Found

Lost in utter darkness, seeking a treasure I could not find, hidden in plain sight. Tormented by poor decisions I've made in my life. Being an outcast—my family's black sheep. I heard a whispered voice saying, "Be of good courage, and I will strengthen your heart." Still confused, I stumbled deeper into a pit of destruction, tearing apart relationships with everyone who once cared—friends, parents and my children.

I cried out with a plea for help, hearing the voice, again, saying, "I will not leave you nor forsake you, I will be with you always." Hope springs within through an overcast of doubt. Doubt, which had me drowning in bitterness and hatred, always seeking revenge.

I've found the treasure, which eluded me all these years. Understanding when the voice says, "I know the thoughts I have towards you, of peace and not evil. To give you a future and a hope." Finer than silver, more precious than platinum or gold, God has given me peace to my soul.

Bradley

" Let my heart be broken with the things that break God's heart. "

— Bob Pierce,
World Vision Founder

A Broken Heart

They say that she died of a heart attack. He believes it was a broken heart. She gave her son every advantage and opportunity that any child could want. He took her love for granted.

He's thirteen years old and leaving for school on a Friday morning, carrying a gym bag full of clothes, not one book. After school, he went straight to the bank, pulled out just enough to get through the weekend. He was headed to kick it with the homies. Gets to his friend's house and they lie to his mother. His parents said it's cool if he spends the night, if it's okay with you. She says yes, so let the weekend begin. Sometime around eleven o'clock that night, he sees his mother's car turn the corner. She's looking for him. He hides, as his homies lie to his Mother. "Have you seen my son?" she asks. "No Ma'am, not since school let out today." He could hear the worry and concern in her voice. "Please tell him that I'm looking for him. Tell him to please come home, if you see him." When she pulls away, he comes out, laughs with his friends as they continue getting high. His thoughts—he is at home. He's with his homies.

Early Monday morning he went home, two maybe three o'clock. He cracks open the front door trying not to wake anyone. Before he reaches the stairs, there's a knock at the door loud enough to wake the dead. He rushes to the door thinking it's his homies bringing him something he forgot. He opens the door to find the police standing there. Quickly he slams the door and turns as a light pops on. Another knock at the door as he looks up to see his mother at the top of the stairs, tears in her eyes. She tells him, "Open the door. It's for you." He opens the door, and one of the officers takes a step inside to ensure that the door won't slam again. He hears his mother coming up behind him; the police have his picture in their hand. The female officer speaks to his mother, "I see he made it home." Gently he feels his mother's hands on his shoulders as she slowly embraces him. "Yes, he's home."

I broke my mother's heart! -Bradley

"The gospel is only good news if it gets there in time."

— Carl F. H. Henry

How the Chicken Crossed the Road

A lot has been said of how we came to faith and repentance. One teaching says, "I chose of my own free will." Another says, "I was chosen outside of my will." Both of these have positive and negative outlooks, depending on the perspective of whom you ask.

The Former:
Positive = that God so loved me that He gave me the freedom to choose.
Negative = I, in my self-righteousness, am saying I saved myself.

The Latter:
Positive = that God so loved me that He picked up out of the pit I could not save myself from.
Negative = that we're robots who are not free.

This is my testimony and confession of the power and glory of God in my life and of how He has brought forth both of these teachings in my conversion. This is how this chicken got to the other side.

Part I
Romans 8:7-8; Genesis 6:5; Psalm 51:4-5; Psalm 58:3
My life, a year prior to my calling, was the poster child for a sinful man. It truly grieves me now to look back and see it all—the drug abuse, more than half my life in prison, and how I ruined people's lives. I hurt the ones I said I loved to an extent I am still ashamed of. I was hateful. I was an adulterer. I was a liar and a thief. I did not honor God or my parents. I made an idol of myself and of a gang lifestyle. My world consisted of me, myself and I.

A monster. I was a slave to sin. Even the moments where I tried to do what I perceived was "good," really were only a delay for my eventual return to sin. My good deeds were about my selfish desires, not for the people I supposedly cared for. Even my best actions were filthy rags.

I was in bondage to Satan and sin. I had the free will to choose how to get high or to pretend I was doing well, but underneath, I was plotting sin. I was blind, deaf, and dumb to spiritual goodness. My will was just a slave.

Part II
John 6:44; Psalm 40:1-3
Everyone, at one point or another, will find ourselves in a place called rock-bottom. Some of us are lucky enough to wake up and find ourselves there. I was not one of these people. This chicken fully face-planted, lip skidded and scorpioned into it.

I was back in prison, losing my marriage and back into addiction. I was so filled with hurt, hate and loss that death seemed a pleasant option compared to dealing with what was inside.

But there is one upside to hitting rock-bottom. It's that your self-righteousness and pride get crushed on impact, and God, in His infinite love, took mercy on me. He put a Christian family in my life who loved me unconditionally, who honestly cared and believed in me. He put me in a prison that has the strongest chapel and pastor I've ever seen. He put a lost friend back in my life, one who just happens to now be a Christian. God also gave me a new best friend, one I could grow and find my way with.

All of these people loved me, stayed with me, dried my tears and protected me. These were all gracious gifts from God that slowly awakened me from that slumber of death. Enabling me to hear and see spiritual goodness for the very first time. Not only see and hear, but to know that I could be a part of it as well.

Part III
John 9:25; Galatians 4:7; Isaiah 43:1-7
God brought me to Kairos at R. J. Donovan Correctional Facility (Kairos #100), where He sat me next to a man who was to become a father, a brother and a mentor in my life. He helped me see my bondage to my sin nature and the lies that the devil had told me my entire life. God used my mentor to bring me to a face-to-face encounter with our Savior, Jesus Christ.

> ❝*In looking at my conversion, yes, I chose Christ as my Savior, and I chose to believe. But it was God who brought me to a point where I could.*❞

My heart was now not one of stone, nor was I blind or deaf to the Holy Spirit. My "free will" was now truly free, and I chose eternal life with God through Christ. On October 24, 2014, I gave myself over to Christ and surrendered to His will. On that day, I was washed clean of my past and baptized by the Holy Spirit, sealed and made a new creation.

Now, I'm a servant of God, an heir of the Kingdom. Fear and death no longer have a hold on me, and I will never again walk on wicked paths. By the grace of God, I have been saved, not of my own doing, but by His will and mercy.

In looking at my conversion, yes, I chose Christ as my Savior, and I chose to believe. But, it was God who brought me to a point where I could. It was His actions in my life that took the scales from my eyes. Where would I be if He had not had mercy on me? While I was still an enemy, He poured gracious gifts into my life. Who would I be, if not for that?

For me, in what the Lord has revealed to me in my walk and through scripture, I've come to this: I was a slave to sin (Romans 8:7-8) and my only will was to serve the devil (John 8:44). I had been that way from the start (Psalm 58:3). My "free will" was there, but held captive and blind. God brought me to a place of brokenness, so that I could see (John 9:25). He drew me to His Son (John 6:44) and revealed the truth, so that my will would truly be free, and I could then choose salvation and become a son (Gal. 4:7). And for me, I could never refuse him nor reject His gift of grace. That is how powerful He is in my life. His call wasn't a whisper—it shook my soul.

To close, I believe that it is to the Lord that all credit goes. Not to the choice I made, but that I only have the free will to make that choice because of God.

Of course, this only scratches the surface of it all. This conversation leads to many others. But, for now, this chicken will be content with this crossed road.

By Brother Jay

I Almost Died That Night

My name is Parker. I grew up in Azusa, CA in LA County. I grew up with both of my parents, who loved me and provided for my every need. Then one day, out of nowhere, when I was in fourth grade, me and my little sister were put in foster care for a false accusation against my father. We came home six months later, but I was a different kid. I was angry, because they took me away. I started tagging, stealing and fighting. I grew up in a gang-infested area but never joined a gang. I thought it was stupid, because I already had a family. I would steal from the mall, K-Mart, any store or person I could. I fought a lot and loved to vandalize.

My parents started fighting a lot. My dad was a drug addict and my mom a drunk. I started smoking cigarettes, marijuana and drinking alcohol at age twelve. I smoked weed every day after that. I loved it. It was my life. I always got in huge trouble every time I drank, though. I could not handle my alcohol. Every time I've been arrested, I've been drunk. I got arrested for possessing weed in 8th grade, and for selling weed in 9th grade, both while at school. I got put in a Christian, military boot camp at age fifteen. I started off in a hard rebellion, cussing and fighting the pastor and my dad. But something ended inside of me.

Me and my friend, Alan, fasted for three days, and they took us to a Christian festival. I went up to the altar call, and I received Jesus in my heart, right then and there. I ended up back in the world shortly after. I ran away and ended up in a sober living home, where I smoked meth for the first time, my first night there. I got hooked and messed up all through high school. I went to seven different high schools and joined a tagging crew. But I graduated. One day, I quit everything—drugs, friends. I isolated myself. I was severely depressed, and I started to hear voices. I punched holes in the walls and through windows. I attacked my dad's roommates. They called the cops. I ended up in a mental hospital with a fourteen-day hold. A short time later, I ended up in county jail, only a few months after turning eighteen and graduating high school. I was mentally ill and still hearing voices. I would bang my head against the walls and fight random people for no reason. I eventually got on medication six months later and slowly got better. The voices went away. I had extremely vivid and disturbing dreams. I paroled after eighteen months and went right back to the same old stuff—tagging crew, meth, drinking, partying like crazy and stealing all kinds of alcohol. I'm lucky I didn't die from drunk driving.

> "*I almost died that night. I couldn't breathe. I woke up gasping for my breath.*"

I ended up attempting suicide. I was severely depressed. I overdosed on sleeping medication. I took a whole bottle. I ended up in an urgent care room getting my stomach pumped. I slept for three days after they pumped my stomach. I ended up back in county jail doing a parole violation. I prayed to God to let me out for Christmas, because I knew in my heart that it would be my last, out, for a long time. I got out for Christmas but ended up back in jail for another violation two months later. I was attacking my family now and stealing everything I could find, drug crazed and depressed. On this second violation, I ended up going to Chino State Prison.

I ended up in a cell with a Satanist. I almost died that night. I couldn't breathe. I woke up gasping for my breath. My cellie woke up. My nose was so clogged up from snorting pills. I ended up leaving, the first chance I had, to the gym. I found God in that gym. I don't know how it happened. I ended up studying the Bible, as a new believer in Christ. I had brothers teaching me. We would pray and sing praise songs all day, every day. I got off all psych meds for the first time.

II Timothy 1:7 was the verse that changed my life. I memorized it and meditated on it. "For God did not give you a spirit of fear, but of power, and of love and of a sound mind." I ended up paroling home a new man. No drugs, no cussing, no smoking, no drinking. I brought my family to church with me. I joined a drug rehab group called the "James Club" which used the Bible and AA book together. I got my first job. Life was good, until I lost my job for lying on my application about my record. It broke me. I gave in to one little compromise. I smoked weed. Then I gave in to one more. I got drunk. Then I smoked meth. I was back in my depressive, hopeless state of being. I had no direction, no purpose. I prayed that God would let me go away for a while in order to grow and mature into a man. I was lost. He put the number eleven on my heart. It felt right. It felt good. I felt like everything would be ok. I still didn't get it, though. I continued to drink to oblivion and drive.

One day, I did something horrible that I regret deeply. I went to jail. I was only out for three months. I ended up with eleven years in state prison. I was angry and destructive. I landed at R. J. Donovan Correctional Facility in 2008. I was drinking and drugging and fighting like there was no tomorrow. I didn't care. I was so angry and hard hearted. I ended up using a needle, and I hit an all-time low. I started practicing Satanism. I hated God. I cursed Him and blasphemed His name. I hated Christians. Then somebody invited me to a 4-day retreat called Kairos. I heard there was unlimited cookies, so I went. I was very rebellious at first. I was bitter and miserable, and for what? Everyone else was having so much fun—loving one another, singing, dancing, laughing.

> " I stopped fighting it and I received the Holy Spirit and all that poison left me. I felt so free. I found such peace and joy. "

Something broke inside of me on the second day. I gave up and gave in. I stopped fighting it, and I received the Holy Spirit, and all that poison left me. I felt so free. I found such peace and joy. God's love penetrated my heart. I didn't want to be that old man anymore. I hated him, and I hated my past, and I hated the world. I hated Satan. I hated sin. I loved God. I felt a second chance given to me. I could be who God wanted me to be. That old man was dead. My past was gone. I was a completely new person. Freedom, peace, purpose, hope, faith, love, joy. I loved my new life in Jesus. II Corinthians 5:17, "Therefore, if anyone is in Christ, he is a new creation; old things have passed away, behold, all things have become new." He has set me free from all my old chains. I have been growing and maturing so much here on C Yard.

> *I am truly saved by grace alone. I do not deserve His mercy. I was a sinner deserving God's wrath and punishment for my sin.*

I feel God's hand moving in other people's lives. I felt God's hand moving in me throughout my life, and I felt it was always His plan to bring me here to this yard to recover my life and what I have lost. God is working through Pastor Roger Ziegler and all the volunteers here at the Church on the Rock. I am now in college, in a seminary class called T.U.M.I., learning to be a minister of Christ Jesus. I am in a self-confrontation class, learning to be counseled and to counsel, using the Bible as the sole authority. I am learning to evangelize and share my faith with the world through "The Way of the Master" course. I am on the praise and worship team here at our church. I love God and am so grateful that He snatched me out of the world and chose me for salvation through faith in His Son, my Lord and Savior, Jesus Christ. I am truly saved by grace alone. I do not deserve His mercy. I was a sinner, deserving God's wrath and punishment for my sin. I broke His law. But by faith in Jesus Christ, I am declared righteous and saved from God's just wrath.

Because of what Jesus did on that cross, He took my punishment. We will all face a judgment day. Hebrews 9:27 "and it is appointed for men to die once, but after this the udgment." Where will you stand on judgment day? Do you have an advocate? Acts 4:12 says "nor is there salvation in any other, for there is no other name under heaven given among men by which we must be saved." If you have broken just one of God's laws, you are in danger of hell fire. Have you ever told a lie? No matter how small? Have you ever stolen anything, no matter the cost? Romans 3:23 say "for all have sinned and fall short of the glory of God." Today is the day of salvation, tomorrow is never promised. Repent, and turn from your sins. What are you waiting for? Jesus is coming soon!

In the name of Jesus,
Parker

" And we know that God causes everything to work together for the good of those who love God and are called according to his purpose for them. "

Romans 8:28

Walking in the Light

1 John 1: 7, "But if we walk in the light, as he is in the light, we have fellowship with one another, and the blood of Jesus Christ His Son cleanseth us from sin."

1 John 1:8, "If we say that we have no sin, we deceive ourselves, and His truth is not in us."

1 John 1:9, "If we confess our sins, he is faithful and just to forgive us our sins, and cleanse us from all unrighteousness."

> **He snatched me out of the world and chose me for salvation through faith in His Son, my Lord and Savior Jesus Christ.**

1 John 1:10, "If we say we have not sinned, we make him a liar, and His word is not in us."

As a way of illustrating my understanding of us as fallible beings and subject to the cares of this world and all it pertains as we make our way in it, I present this poor illustration.

Back when I was a young boy, my step-dad and grandfather used to gather up the dogs at 3:00 am in the sticks of Porterville to go rabbit hunting. Naturally, me being the eldest of the boys, it was the high point of my summer vacation to go tearing off through the sticks in the back hills with Granddad, those dogs and real guns. There was just no higher privilege than that; I was on cloud nine.

So after swearing up and down to them that I would be able to keep up, off we went before sunrise.

We would carry one kerosene lantern. My granddad, leading, would carry that lantern, and it was dark as a dungeon in those sticks that early in the morning. So, I would position myself right behind my Granddad who had the light. I was fairly afraid of the dark.

But as the hunt wore on and we climbed through the bushes, I would grow tired, and my short legs would begin to fail me, and I would fall behind and out of the light of that lantern. I would trash around in the brush and run into the limbs, and by the time I caught up to Dad and Grandpa, I would be a mess—all scratched and bruised up and wishing I was back home, safe.

But my Granddad's foot would never falter. He would stop and listen for the dogs and then go on. He knew what it was about and where he was, but I was totally lost without the light of that lantern.

> **"We are not to judge those people whom we see staggering in darkness. It may be us that gets out of the light next."**

It is that way with walking in the light of the Spirit. We grow tired soon, and we begin to look around. Our footsteps falter, and we get out of the light. Then we get scratched up, bruised and tattered by this world and the sin in it, so we run to catch up to Jesus, our blessed Redeemer.

Sometimes, I would get out of the light of that lantern and fall right into a hole in the ground, because I could no longer see clearly. I would fall prostrate and just end up fighting the bushes. I would get desperate to reach that lantern light.

Have you seen a Christian thrashing around in a hole? Have you ever been in one yourself?

We are not to judge those people whom we see staggering in darkness. It may be us that gets out of the light next.

f we walk in the light as He is in the light, we are well. Unfortunately, we lag behind, so we get in and out of that light, and that is when we get all bruised up, dirty and bleeding, spiritually speaking. When I would go stumbling around and get in too big a mess, my granddad would pick me up and carry me on his broad shoulders for a while. Then, after a while, he would sit me back down and say, "There now," and it made me feel good, because he cared.

That is sort of like it is with Jesus. He sometimes just picks us up and carries us. If I could always just walk in the Spirit, walk in the light as He is in the light, it would be great. But I don't always do that, and so I get bruised, scratched up, worn-out, tattered and torn by the sins that so easily beset me, while living in this flesh. Oh, my spirit is all too willing, but the flesh is all too weak.

So, before we pass judgment on those Christians that do seem to have fallen in a hole, we best ask ourselves what hole we are subject to falling into. We are all just big children, and we are subject to falter. Some just more than others. So, I believe it was Paul who said, "Walk in the Spirit and you will not fulfill the lust of the flesh." He knew we would not always be able to do that.

So, to those that are walking in the Spirit, let's pray for those who falter. We need to encourage one another to "run and catch up to Jesus, our light, in this dark world."

There are so many precious promises in His word and words of encouragement. He made us the promise that He would never leave us nor forsake us. And friend, I have found that to be true in my thrashing around through the mountains and valleys and the bushes and brambles of this life.

I leave you with these final scriptures:
"But you, beloved, building yourselves up on your most holy faith, praying in the Holy Spirit." Jude 1:20

"Keep yourselves in the love of God, looking for the mercy of our Lord Jesus Christ unto eternal life." Jude 1:21

"And on some have compassion, making a distinction." Jude 1:22

"But on others save with fear, pulling them out of the fire, hating even the garment defiled by the flesh." Jude 1:23

We need to watch over one another in love, know how to make a difference between the weak and the willful, and act accordingly.

A very strong and wise brother, "Beloved," once told me, "As iron sharpens iron, so shall men sharpen men."

A brother in Christ,
Richard

" You are the light of the world. A town built on a hill cannot be hidden. Neither do people light a lamp and put it under a bowl. Instead they put it on its stand, and it gives light to everyone in the house. In the same way, let your light shine before others, that they may see your good deeds and glorify your Father in heaven. "

Matthew 5:13-16

" How can a young
man keep his
way pure?
By living according
to your word. "

Psalm 119:9

Out of the Darkness and Into the Light, My Walk from Sadness to Salvation

My name is Johnny. I am forty-one years old and I have been incarcerated for the better part of my teenage and adult life.

Before I tell you about some of my past, I would like to tell you why I am writing this letter. It has been a goal of mine to work with at-risk youth once I am released from prison, and I would like to do so, with the guidance of Jesus Christ our Savior.

> *As I look back and reflect on my life, I wish I had someone to speak to that is coming from the place I am now.*

My release date from prison is under two years. I know it would be easy for me to just set my sails and sail off into my life of freedom, but that is not something I see myself doing. That would be very selfish of me to waste the life I have lived, by placing it into some kind of box and never sharing my journey. I was once that little boy that was taken from my home and placed in Juvenile Hall, locked in a cell, wondering why my family did not love me enough to come and save me. I was once that scared little boy, sitting in the back of cars, heading off to group homes, one after the other, never knowing how long each stay would last.

As I look back and reflect on my life, I wish I had someone to speak to that is coming from the place I am now. If so, I don't think I would have spent my entire adult life in California's prison system.

At the ripe age of seventeen, with adulthood around the corner, I saw myself walking down the path of becoming a gang member. It started with me just hanging out with my buddies and then got serious when I found a group I felt at home with. I am from the Bay area, and in 1988, I become a full member of a skinhead squad called B.A.S.H. (Bay Area Skinheads). That decision took me to State Prison by my twentieth birthday. Once in prison, I became known to a white supremacist prison gang and decided to see what it had to offer.

> " *I found that the old saying was true, what goes up must always come down.* "

I paroled from C.D.C. in 1997, and within a year, I almost beat a man to death at a party, thus being convicted of nine felonies and given the prison sentence of twenty years at 85%. At that point, my life changed once again. I was moving up that ladder of the criminal and gang life. I was shipped off to Corcoran State Prison to begin a life of being housed on level four yards and ending up housed in Corcoran S.H.U. (Security Housing Unit). I found myself committing crimes worse than the crime I was sent to prison for. I saw no hope in my life, and with being so lost, managed to continue moving up that ladder of gang life.

In May 2002, I found that my time had come to pay for all my deeds. I found that the old saying was true, "what goes up must always come down." My fall from the ladder was hard. Prison politics had caught up with me, and I found that I was not willing to spend my entire life locked in a cell deep inside Corcoran S.H.U., as I once thought I was. After some time to think, I decided it was time to leave the "Game." In doing so, I had to lock up and debrief. I became the type of person that I despised. However, I knew that if I had stayed, I eventually would have to pay with my life, by getting hit or receiving a life sentence. Honestly, I don't know what would have been worse.

A year later, in 2003, I was diagnosed with cancer. I came out of that and went into remission. I pushed on with my life in prison but was not housed in a yard designed for ex-gang members. Despite leaving, I was still doing drugs, fighting and filled with hate. I was still the same person, just housed differently.

June 26, 2009 my world fell apart. I had called home to find out that my mother had passed away in her sleep. I had known she was sick, but she had hidden how bad it was, because she didn't want me to worry. That day I got high and stayed that way for three full years. A beast was inside of me that I could not control. He was very big and very violent. I found myself doing anything to take the pain away, to cover the shame of being a bad son—the type that would leave his mother to die in her sleep without me near. My mother now lives with God.

Now, something about my religious beliefs: Since the time of becoming a skinhead, I was taught a Northern European religion called Asatru (Odinism). It is based on the Norse myths, the Viking Gods. Being a skinhead, this all tied into being a racist. At this time of my life, I had been an Odinist for about 16 years. I used this as a platform for hate and to recruit new members into the game.

In May 2012, after a long battle with the medical department here at C.D.C., I was told that my cancer had returned, and I would need yet another surgery to save my life. Back in 2003, I had testicular cancer and had one of them removed to save my life. Now, here I am close to ten years later, and they're telling me that I have to do this again.

At this point in my life, I was still using drugs and very angry, because I had been telling them I did not feel good for about a year. When I arrived at the prison in 2008, I was weighing in at 230 lbs., at 6'2, and in very good shape. Now I was 165 lbs., and very angry.

On July 23, 2012, my cell door opened, and at about three in the morning, I was told to get ready, transportation would pick me up soon. I was put in a van and taken to Alvarado Hospital. I was prepared to do what needed to be done, once again. Everything was fine. Then, I remember being on that gurney and rolling down that hallway. It seemed like it was miles long and the lights were so bright. It seemed like it took an hour to get into the operating room. This is where my life changed forever.

> **"*I just wanted to tell her how I loved her so much.*"**

I looked over at a clock on the wall, and as I focused on the hands of the clock, the second hand stopped moving. At this point they were already trying to put me to sleep. I freaked out and tried to get off the table; prison guards were there to prevent an escape attempt. I knew if I allowed them to put me to sleep, I would die. I began to cry, like I had only one other time in my life—when my mother had died. I felt the rage coming inside me. I was prepared to hurt anyone to get off that table. Then, right in the middle of all this madness, I heard my mom's voice. It was like all the wind was knocked out of me, and I lay back on the table. I looked over at the clock, and the second hand was moving again. I will never forget my mom's words to me, "Baby, don't fight. You will be okay." I wish I could have laid there and talked to my mom forever. I would have told her how sorry I am for wasting my life, for tattooing my whole body, for the drugs and violence. I just wanted to tell her how I loved her so much. At that very moment, I prayed to God to save my life, and I swore to Jesus Christ that I would not waste another day of this life that He gives me. I never believed in God before this day. My mother brought me to Jesus three years after she joined Him in heaven.

The day, July 23, 2012 at 8:15 in the morning, the old me died. The skinhead, the racist, the Odinist, the liar, the criminal, the drug addict and the thief—they all died. I was reborn and found Jesus Christ, then I accepted Him as my Savior. Since that day, my life has been blessed. My cancer is gone, never to return. I have a great pastor to mentor me, and I have found peace on a prison yard. I have found brothers in Christ that have always been here. I have a beautiful lady in my life who also believes in God. I plan to spend the rest of my life with her, if she will have me. I have begun to build my new life on a foundation prepared by God. I base my entire walk on God and Jesus Christ. Now my life has become easy. I am blessed for the first time in twenty years. The weight of the world has lifted off my shoulders. Since that day, I go to church, and I pray every day. I place any problems I have in the hands of God. I am aware of the plan that God has for me.

I want to help take the next generation of gang members away from C.D.C.R. I was once that scared little boy. Now, I want to be the hand to lift that next little boy up. May God bless you and your family. I keep all the brothers and sisters in Christ in the free world in my prayers.

With God's Love, Johnny

Update from Johnny...

After being out for almost a year now, I have been adjusting well. At first, it was hard; but as long as I stood strong and faithful, I knew the Lord would bless me and help guide me on the right path.

Soon after getting out, I got a job. It wasn't in the industry I wanted, but I knew I had to support my wife and I. After a few months with that company, I found a different job that helped my wife and I financially, but it still wasn't the job I wanted and craved for.

During this time, my wife and I were searching for a home church to attend. We went to a couple. One was too big, and I knew it would be hard to develop a relationship with the pastor the way I had with Pastor Roger Zeigler. The second church was smaller; but, unfortunately, my wife and I didn't feel at home or very welcomed there. Although these churches had good intentions, there still wasn't that feeling I had when I attended the Church on the Rock at the R. J. Donovan Correctional Facility.

Even though I struggled to find our home church, I still stayed strong in my faith and continued in my walk with Christ. During this time, my wife and I were invited by a Kairos volunteer to give my testimony at his church. Brother Pete Mendoza and his pastor made me feel more than welcome and gave me a chance to share my recovery with the church. Upon returning home, I was determined to not only find a home church, but also to get back into the industry I loved so much, towing.

After a lot of struggles, I managed to get my foot in the door and had a plan as to how I was going to get this dream job. I went in for an interview with my mind set that I would not mention being on parole. If they asked about it, I had decided to lie and tell them NO. But God, being the Almighty that He is, would not allow it and decided it was time for a lesson on grace.

On that day, I was blessed to meet Dino and Andrea Tomassi, the people God placed in my life to help me learn a lesson on grace. The question did, in fact, come up about me being on parole, and with my game plan set, I lied. Dino and Andrea were not fooled. They kept drilling me, asking these questions in hopes I would slip up. Instead, I asked to start the interview over, because a look in their eyes let me know they knew I was keeping something from them. I started out by telling them that, yes, I was, in fact, on parole, and I explained to them why I lied.

> **"** *Mrs. Andrea Tomassi looked me straight in the eye and said, 'we believe in grace.'* **"**

The interview went on, and I felt that I had not only let myself and wife down, but also God. As the interview was coming to an end, and I was walking out the door feeling defeated, something inside me told me to go back and ask for a favor from Dino and Andrea. I asked if they would watch my testimony on YouTube, so they could not only see why I was so scared to tell them about my situation, but also so they could see my character and the truth about who I am today. Before I left, after making that request, Mrs. Andrea Tomassi looked me straight in the eye and said, "We believe in grace."

A couple of days later, I received a call from Finish Line Towing. It was Andrea asking me to come in and discuss some possibilities. With hope in my heart, my faith strong, and my wife supporting me, I was more than happy to go in, but not without my folder of certificates I earned while involved with the Kairos community. I walked through their door nervous, yet hopeful. Dino and Andrea welcomed me into their family that day and explained, again, to me how they believe in grace. They explained that after watching my testimony, they not only wanted me, but felt in their hearts that I would be a great addition to the Finish Line Towing family. As we went over my paper work, Andrea was asking about other programs I was involved in while at RJD. With a great big smile, I pulled out my folder with all my certificates, and proudly showed them to her. As she was looking through them, she saw my many certificates from Celebrate Recovery. To my surprise, Andrea informed me that her and Dino were also involved in CR at their church, Bridges Community Church in Fremont, CA. My eyes grew big, and with that reaction, Dino and Andrea invited my wife and I to their church and to join them for the Celebrate Recovery group, which they both run.

> ❝ *Through His strength I see that all things are possible and by that I live my life.* ❞

My wife and I now have a home church, and our faith is stronger than ever now. God has truly blessed me since He saved me, and He has shown me, as long as I remain faithful, He will continue to do so. Since working for Dino, he has decided to help make this job into a career. He took it upon himself to send and pay for my schooling, so I can grow with his company and the Finish Line Towing family. I now work full-time and also go to school. I am staying busy and out of trouble, and I am making a positive impact on those around me. My parole officer is proud of me, something I never thought would happen, and she refers to me as her "ray of sunshine."

All things are possible through Christ. I really see that now, going from an everyday sinner to this strong, Christian man has shown me the power of our Savior. God has had a plan for me from day one. First, He needed me to struggle and feel lost, not knowing He was there for me the whole time, just so when I found Him and His amazing love, He would be able to give me a glimpse of all the great things He has always had planned for me. Through His strength, I see that all things are possible, and by that I live my life. Philippians 4:13

" Have no part at all in the wrong things that young men like to do. Believe. Have love. Follow what is right. Live at peace. Do these things along with others who have a clean heart and talk to God. "

2 Timothy 2:22-25

" And without faith
it is impossible to
please God, because
anyone who comes to
him must believe
that he exists and
that he rewards
those who earnestly
seek him. "

Hebrews 11:6

Does God Exist?

I came to Kairos on October 25, 2014 as a non-believer. It's not that I didn't believe in a Christian God, I simply didn't believe in any god. You see, I was a "skinhead," and most of my friends were Odinists.

I came to Kairos at the request of a former skinhead who is now a Christian. He called in a debt so to speak! We met way back in 1997 at Folsom State Prison, where I was fresh out of the S.H.U. (Segregated Housing Unit) at Corcoran State Prison, where I had been given the power and authority over the skinheads within the prison. I had called on this former skinhead "David" at this time and he came knowing the potential danger that he was being put in. Now, here we are many years later at R. J. Donovan Correctional Facility, where David reminded me of our past. Using it for good, he called me to Christ and reminded me of the danger that I had put him in, but he told me that Kairos would not pose any threat or danger to me. I felt it was a fair request, so I went. You see, David had just been given a release date by the Board of Prison Hearings, and he was to go home prior to my Kairos event.

> ❝His trust and faith in Jesus Christ never wavered. ❞

David expressed to me his concern that he wanted me to go, even though he would not be there. He didn't know at the time that the governor would be reversing his parole grant, thus losing his date. Being in prison for over twenty years, this news was a tremendous disappointment to him, yet his trust and faith in Jesus Christ never wavered.

Seeing this brother respond as he did, and knowing that there is a worldwide belief in God, I made the promise to myself to go to Kairos. I would take this seriously, with only one question in mind. I wanted to find out, "Does God exist?"

Kairos, Day 1 - Orientation and introduction. "Hi, my name is Guy. I don't believe in God. My favorite pastime is taking naps. You see, I've got a life sentence, so sleep is my escape." Little did I know, I made myself the subject of interest to everyone within the chapel. There were approximately seventy-five men in that room, mostly all believers, at different stages within their faith. So, I figured, with all these people here, whether inmates or volunteers, laymen or clergy, somebody is bound to have the answer to my simple question, "How do I come to believe in God?"

I'd like to bring something to everyone's attention. I've come to believe that people take the mere belief in God for granted. What I mean by this is, when you are young, going to church or Sunday School, one grows up with the innate belief that God does exist. He's always there! If you happen to drift away from your faith, you know deep within that you can turn back to Him, and He will be there. Now, here I am, not having that type of foundation, an adult not having faith nor belief of any kind. An example would be that of a Native American who had never seen a car. He has no concept of a car and what you are trying to convey to him, yet all you have to do is show him a car, and now he believes. The same goes for me. Having never seen God, how can you show me God? I needed to see God!

> "Man of them had similar backgrounds such as I, walking with many hurts and pains which I was able to relate to."

The first day of Kairos went well enough. I found myself in the center of an intense storm of singing and dancing to songs that I had never heard before. I listened to inspirational talks, many of them from the Bible, which again, I knew nothing about. I intermingled with the volunteers, as they shared their personal testimonies and stories of faith. Many of them had similar backgrounds such as mine, walking with many hurts and pains, which I was able to relate to. However, my question still remained, and by the end of the day, still t was unanswered. I spoke with several of the volunteers, and they all said the same thing, "Accept Jesus Christ." You don't understand, I don't believe in God! I was looking for the process, a formula, so to speak. I just wanted to know what had to do. One guy told me that I was over-thinking it, and another engaged in the battle over me, never giving up on me. Day after day, he stayed on me until I gave in, opening the door of my heart just enough for Jesus to reveal Himself to me. At the end of the first day, I was a little shocked that I did not get the nice, simple and easy answer that I was looking for. Instead, I was left tossing and turning in bed, spending a great deal of energy, thinking about God. Keep in mind that I did not know how to pray, but yet, this is exactly what I was doing, without even knowing it. Spending time with God is exactly what we all need to do more often.

On day two, as I'm heading back to the chapel, my friend comes by to ask me if I had found the answer to my question. He did this for the next three days. He shared with me a concept that he had come up with. He said, "Picture yourself on a sidewalk, looking at a door in the distance that you need to get to. There is grass between the sidewalk and the door. When you first look at the grass there are no stepping stones, but as you take the first step, a stepping stone appears. That's God. He is the solid foundation that will begin your journey in Him." So, I closed my eyes, relaxed and concentrated all my thoughts on Him as I took that first step. I actually took that step, and something clicked. I could see, like a movie, myself opening that door to Jesus.

I've got to admit that Kairos is supposed to be an enjoyable experience, and I believe that most people do have a great time singing, dancing, hearing stories and eating home baked cookies. After all, what's not great about that? But for me, it was a natural beating. I didn't know the songs, couldn't dance, not to mention I was busy thinking about how or when

I was going to get my elusive question answered. Since 1976, I've only been on the streets thirty-three months, and believe me, prison food sucks, so the cookies made for an awesome treat. However, with little to no sleep, Kairos was a difficult experience for me.

There were several symbolic exercises that we did, which really helped me remove the heavy load that I had been carrying for many years. One of them was the "Forgiveness Ceremony." It lifted a great weight and gave me such a great sense of newfound peace.

On the fourth day is when I accepted Jesus into my life. Pastor Roger invited us all up to accept Christ and to receive a cross around our necks. As my turn approached, Roger said to me, "Christ is counting on you," and my response was, "and I am counting on Christ." As the weight of the cross hit my chest, a profound feeling came across me like I had never felt before. I actually felt a physical tap or sensation that shot from the cross to my chest and into my back. It was a physical, yet spiritual, touch at the same time.

I've spent my whole life surrounded by concrete and steel. If someone would have told me about having this experience, I wouldn't have believed them. Yet, here I stand today, telling you that God has broken down these hardened walls, and I'm now a new man in Christ. It is real! It's humbled me and broke me down in front of a room full of men and women.

I am here today to tell you, God is real! He does exist! I met Him at Kairos 100 in maximum security prison. His agape love filled my heart, and all He asked me to do is love Him back, with everything that is in me, to love others with that same love, and to just keep it simple!

God bless, Guy

" When I was a child, I spoke like a child, I thought like a child, I reasoned like a child. When I became a man, I put aside childish things. "

1 Corinthians 13:11

Only Fate

Unexplainably intriguing from one moment to the next
Trust in him as it unfolds
The author of it all, great and small
Patiently knocking on your heart
You've been set apart, found forever more
So live to follow not to figure out
Learning what it is to love God
To follow him through the doubt
When the World's discouragement says that
It won't ever happen or that it's impossible
The fate of Christ will suffice
Written in fate God will set you free from
the problems you create
Only truth will dictate 'cause it's been written in your fate
God has made you great, effective in your own way
Above and not below, the head and not the tail
The Lord will prevail, it's your testimony
His light shines purely, so complete
Christ the ultimate warrior of sacrifice
Through him I am complete
For his word guides my feet

Randall
Winning souls for Christ through fate.

Learning

Twisted branches strangling vines
Agony from past time
Thoughts ache, pain fills the mind
Testing time alive and
Well yet so blinded by pride
Arrogance glimmers and anger shines
Blame surfaces, ignorance defined
Leaving no room for the voice of peace
Ripped and scared from years of abuse
Negative direction continuous
Lack of parental affection growing into an
Insecure complexion and Department of Corrections
Never giving up was an only direction
Losing the way only to learn he would be an
Honorable man living a positive life guided by
God's plan living to follow, not to figure out
Leading by example
Loving God with all your heart you will never go without
Knowing Jesus, that's what it's all about.

Randall

Shattered Dreams

Ink splattered flesh
Track marks explain the rest
The needle and tears a hole
Pain afflicts the soul like changing choices
Create insanity 'cause it'll always be the same
Aching bones and yearning veins
Substance takes the reigns, controlling the same
Blotting out the sun, in circles we run
Out of breath, desperation proves the test
Left with the aching of a broken heart
Sets you apart
A time to think, am I on the brink
Shattered dreams
Not knowing what it means to find joy in everything
Some stand and some fall
Many are overtaken by it all
Choosing, will I win or will I lose
Saved by Christ, so I win because He is
The champion who calls
He has overcome it all
Great and small

Randall

"Watch and pray so that you will not fall into temptation. The spirit is willing, but the body is weak."

Matthew 26:41

"I am the light of the world. Whoever follows me will never walk in darkness, but will have the light of life."

John 8:12

Light was Found Through Jesus Christ

came to prison at the young age of twenty for the ultimate crime of taking a man's life. Up until that time, I was a petty criminal and drug addict, lost in the world, confused about my future. I could not see that my life was leading down a destructive path, because I was so self-centered.

When I landed in prison, I joined a skinhead gang to be accepted and find validation. I believed this was the best path for me to survive in this dark place. Soon after, I was introduced to Asatru ("belief in the gods"). I began to lose myself to some fantasy world that only existed for my own personal gain. As I continued in this life, I hurt people and would drink to forget the things I did on behalf of the "gang." After a while, the person I was as a young boy disappeared, and I didn't even realize it.

In 2009, I ended up getting jumped and stabbed, along with one of my "comrades," in a gang retaliation. I thought I was going to die, and as darkness descended, I felt empty and scared. This impacted me, and when I awoke in the hospital, I began to think seriously about the direction my life was heading and the condition of my soul.

The experience of my near-death left me empty inside. A year later, I left the gang I was in but still held on to my pagan beliefs. Yet, there was a deep emptiness inside of me. I was in so much pain, I did not even realize it. Depression dogged my every step, and I remained in this state, off and on, for about two years.

After continuing with my program, with no clear direction except the desire to change my life for the better, out of nowhere, the medical department classified me "high risk medical care" due to the spinal fracture I suffered when I got jumped. This meant I had to be transferred to a medical facility.

Before I knew it, I was transferred to R. J. Donovan and ran into an old friend who had been in the same gang I had been in. My friend had changed his life and turned it over to Jesus Christ. I thought he was joking with me, but he was serious about his conversion. I was still lost spiritually but had no interest in Christianity. My friend told me about Kairos that is held every six months and invited me to attend. I was hesitant at first, because I wasn't ready to hear any preaching or be bothered by a bunch of Christians trying to convert me.

> "*Everything that happened in my life led me to Him.*"

In the end, I agreed to go for all the cookies I could eat. It was the best thing that ever happened to me. Day one was a shock, because of the LOVE I felt in the room for God. On the second day, I felt my soul stirred and a spark ignited where, before, darkness resided. On the third day, March 16, 2013, I hung up my pagan hammer and put on the cross, giving my life to Jesus Christ. I never believed that I would ever consider it. People have tried sharing the Word with me so many times before, but I continually rebuffed them. God knew me for a rebellious spirit and hard head. Everything that happened in my life led me to Him. The darkness that I had felt, but did not understand, is now filled with the light of a new believer.

Outwardly, the world is the same, but now I see it in a new light. God has given a gift to an unworthy man. This is the power of His Grace that I will never lose sight of. I'm a new man in Christ, growing closer to God and His Word, living to pass on the message of HOPE and LIFE. The life I led was an empty one, until Jesus Christ found me and transformed me. I hope that anyone who is going through their own trials will open up and allow the Word of God into their lives. You will not need drugs, alcohol, gangs or a criminal lifestyle to fill the void you may have in your life.

Sincerely, Steven

" It was good for me to be afflicted so that I might learn your decrees. "

Psalm 119:71

" But rejoice inasmuch as you participate in the sufferings of Christ, so that you may be overjoyed when his glory is revealed. "

1 Peter 4:13

A Sense of Reality

My name is Joshua. I am twenty-three years old and happy, regardless of being in prison.

I grew up in Hollywood, CA. I was raised in a Christian home and had the perfect example of hard working, loving parents. Things seemed perfect, until one day at eight years old, I heard my parents arguing. The next day, there was an awkward silence, and then my parents' marriage ended quickly with a divorce months later. I spent time with my dad on weekends, only due to court orders. I started living with my mom and grandmother. Eventually, both my parents met other people, and I wasn't very comfortable with either one of them. I felt like they were trying to take my mom's and dad's place. I didn't get along with my mom's new husband, but they had a son, and I was happy about having a little brother. Unfortunately, two years later, my stepfather died, and we were left without a father figure in the house. I went to many schools in the area, and because we moved a lot, I would get into trouble. My Mother would wake me up early to get to school, and only the janitor would be there. I would go to church with my mother, but I always felt like something was missing in my life.

When I was twelve, we moved to North Hollywood. Our neighbors introduced me to weed, drinking and gangs. I was hooked. My first bust was at twelve years old, and I was arrested. I was carrying a spray can to do graffiti on walls. My mother was so angry. I became more rebellious, though. On my thirteenth birthday, it became a turning point in my life. I had the choice to enjoy a party my mom arranged, with cake, presents and family, or go with my friends and hang out with a gang. Selfishly, I chose my friends and the gang. I would continue to sneak out of my house, not come home for days, leaving my mother worried, and being a bad example for my little brother. I later robbed a guy walking the streets alone with my friend and served a month in Juvenile Hall for it. We got out with a slap on the hand, and this should have opened my eyes to see the stupidity I was getting into. But instead, I fell even deeper into the gang lifestyle. I ended up in Juvi for three more months, then six months. It started to feel normal to me. I even said I was ready to do time in prison, because I was part of a big gang, and in California prisons, they honored gang members.

I became more and more careless and stubborn. I would say, back then, that I cared for my family and my life, but in all reality, I just cared what my friends and girlfriends thought. My mother asked me one day, "When are you going to change, Mijo?" I'd say, "One day, but not now," just to get her off my case, not realizing that she was praying for me to change. I was on the streets of Hollywood again, drinking and hanging out with my girlfriend. This was against my probation, but I didn't care. That is, until the police showed up, and I ended up being arrested again. When I showed up in court, the judge said, "Oh you're back again," and I ended up with a house arrest and a bracelet on my ankle. As I walked away, looking back at my mother's face, which was very sad, an officer looked at me and told me, "This probably will be your last chance, if you don't change." But I brushed it off and walked out with a grin on my face.

> **" There was blood everywhere. I felt my heart giving out and I said in a whisper, God help me. "**

Again, I ended up living the gang life. I was with my girlfriend, and a van drove up, and a bunch of guys jumped out. I didn't want my girlfriend to get hurt, so I went after them. I ended up getting stabbed with a knife six times—two times in my head, one in my back, two in my ribs and one in my arm. As I continued to fight, I blacked out. When I woke up, no one was around. I stumbled into a local store, grabbed a water and stumbled out. There was blood everywhere. I felt my heart giving out, and I said in a whisper, "God help me." As soon as I said that, I saw my girlfriend come and help me up, and she poured water on my face, head and hands. As we walked towards a friend's house—what seemed to be the longest walk ever—I apologized to my girl for not changing. I told her that I loved her and to not forget about me, if I was going to die. My friends called 911 for an ambulance, as I passed out. When I woke up, I was being treated by the paramedics, as my ex-girlfriend and girl were watching. I thought, "How embarrassing is this?"

> **"I'm here to share my story with you and how Jesus Christ saved me from what you are going through right now in your life."**

I was supposed to be this macho gang member, but look where it got me. They rushed me to the hospital, and I had to go into surgery, as my lungs had collapsed. As I woke up, in and out of consciousness, I saw mostly my family, who loved me in my darkest moments. I dosed off, and when I woke up again, I saw a man at the end of my bed in a wheelchair. I asked him who he was and he told me, "I'm here to share my story with you and how Jesus Christ saved me from what you are going through right now in your life." He told me how he was into gangs, drugs and all that. He got shot in the leg, went into the hospital, got out, then got shot, again, in the arm, and got out of the hospital, yet continued doing his gang banging. Then he got shot a third time, in his back, and was now paralyzed from the legs down. That's when he said he gave up fighting against God and those who truly loved him. He said he gave his life to God, and God changed him. He said he never felt so much peace. In return, I said, "Yeah, I know all about that. I grew up in church with my family." I had no compassion for his story.

I got out of the hospital in a week and a half and left with the house arrest bracelet still on my ankle. My probation officer called and told me, if I didn't get to school, I would be violating my probation and would go back to Juvi. Three weeks later, I asked a friend to bring a 22 rifle to my school. After school, I got the gun. I was looking for trouble, and I found it. We rode into Santa Monica, and someone my friend was arguing with on the streets said a gang name. I felt a panic attack, and I just reacted instantly by pulling out the gun and shooting the guy in the chest. I turned and started to run with the gun at my side. The police found us, saw my house arrest anklet and told me, "We know you shot that guy." It was back to Juvenile Hall, but this time with a murder case.

> **"At 16 years old, facing life in prison for a gang-related murder, I knew this was no joke."**

Even in Juvenile Hall, I was fighting, using drugs and wanted to commit suicide. At sixteen years old, facing life in prison for a gang-related murder, I knew this was no joke. I was transferred to another juvenile hall and there I started going to the church services. I listened to what a lady volunteer said. She asked me if I accepted the Lord Jesus Christ as my Lord and Savior. I said no, and she invited me to do so then. When I went back to my cell, I started to pray, asking God, "I'm here, I don't know what to do anymore with my life. I give my life to you, please change me." At that moment, I was at peace and filled with a hope that I hadn't felt in a long time. People that knew me before I changed would say, "There's something different about you." I would tell them that God had changed me. I'd tell them that I'm done with the gangs, drugs and all the violence. I didn't want that life any more. At eighteen, as I was fighting my case in court, an officer told me I was going to face life in prison. I looked at him and said, "I'm not worried about life in prison, as long as I have eternal life in Jesus." At this time, my trust wasn't in myself, nor the court, or my attorney, but it was in God who changed me.

Over the next few months in prison, I ran into my friend whom I was arrested with. I shared with him how God had changed ne, but it made him angry, and he and some other gang members jumped me. I did not fear them though. I feared God and left my life in His hands. I was jumped five times in different places, and every time God rescued me. When went to my last court date, I was given fifty-years-to-life. The family of the guy I shot came to the stand and said that they forgave me and just wanted justice in my sentencing. It was so sad to see my family and the family of the one whose life I took hurt because of my actions. I knew I wasn't the same person as before. My life goal now is to give back to society, as I'm able. I'm involved in community programs to help struggling youth, I'm taking education classes, and I am still grateful for having a changed heart and life. I continue to grow, learn and be grateful, knowing that one day I'll be released from prison, being a new man, and no longer childish, and ready to help change lives from a wrong path to a right path of life.

Sincerely,
Joshua

Friends

I'm in prison doing life. God helps me overcome fear,
torment and strife.

I read my Bible and I pray. God gives me love, hope
and contentment to get through each day.
I was blind but now I see. I've been redeemed at the cross.
I've been set free.

I'm here to spread God's word. I hope you all believe.
Surrender your life to Jesus Christ and God will set you free.
God's given us the Bible. It's His Word we must believe.
It teaches us about sin and salvation as we read.
We learn about God's Son Jesus and what
He did on the cross for us at Calvary.

We learn if we put our faith in God's Son Jesus,
God will be our Father throughout eternity.

God's love and forgiveness won't be with you in the lake of
fire. Only God's wrath. Unending pain, torment and sorrow.
You won't end up there if you repent. Surrender your life to
Jesus Christ and become born again. John 3:3
Jesus answered and said to him, "Most assuredly I say to you,
unless one is born again he cannot see the
Kingdom of God, amen!"

Listen to the radio, watch TV. Hear the world's expectations.
See the world's views. What goes into our minds can conform
us to what we think and do. We need to tune out the world's
expectations. We need to reject the world's views. We must
read the Bible. Be transformed by the good news.
Put our faith in Jesus Christ. Put our trust in God's views!

I've learned that the riches of this world won't satisfy all
your needs. The emptiness in our hearts can only be filled
by the power of the Holy Spirit through Jesus Christ
with God's love from above!

Brother Ron

The Celebration Song

There's gonna be a celebration when we get to heaven,
There's gonna be a celebration when we see Jesus Christ.
There's gonna be jumping and shouting.
There's gonna be shouting and jumping.
We will be praising God the Father. We will be praising Jesus Christ.
There will be no more death or crying.
There will be no more sadness or sorrow.
We will have everlasting bodies.
There will be no more aches and pains.
There's gonna be a celebration when we get to heaven.
There's gonna be a celebration when we see Jesus Christ.
There' gonna be jumping and shouting.
There's gonna be shouting and jumping.
We will be praising God the Father. We will be praising Jesus Christ.
We will be living in mansions.
We will be walking on streets of gold.
We will be eating from the tree of life in the midst of Paradise.
There's gonna be a celebration when we get to heaven.
There's gonna be a celebration when we see Jesus Christ.
There's gonna be jumping and shouting.
There's going to be shouting and jumping.
We will be praising God the Father. We will be praising Jesus Christ.
We need to be coming together.
We need to be meeting in the house of the Lord.
We need to be reading the Bible.
We need to be spreading the good news.
We need to be telling all the people all about Jesus Christ.
It's all about Jesus, Jesus Christ. It's all about Jesus Christ

But I have trusted in Your mercy. My heart shall rejoice in
Your salvation. I will sing to the Lord because He has dealt
bountifully with me. Psalm 13:5-6

Brother Ron
(I can just hear him singing these now!)

" Dear brothers and sisters, if another believer is overcome by some sin, you who are godly should gently and humbly help that person back onto the right path. And be careful not to fall into the same temptation yourself. "

Galatians 6:1

Hidden Treasure, My Heart

Thick stone imprisoned a vital organ. Rage, fear and hate creating this unbreakable barrier, no longer feeling for others. Destruction my primary focus, a twister destroying trailer park homes. Debris left in my wake, never thinking of consequences. Numerous attempts to break the stone finally proves worthy. Terror grips me as a fear of the unknown takes over, forgetting the power of this vital organ. Of all the attempts spiritual principles prove the best route. A whack of my chisel with kindness creates a dent. Compassion and honesty sprawl chips of stone. Chipping away at this rocky barrier, love the greatest blow. The force exploding enormous amounts of stone exposing a soft center. The final blow of empathy unveils a vibrant blood red pulsating orb. Long forgotten from childhood, memories take over. My eyes begin to water as emotions of love, kindness, compassion and empathy fill this hidden treasure, my heart.

Nicholas

" Sin is not weakness,
it is a disease;
it is red-handed
rebellion against God
and the magnitude
of that rebellion is
expressed by
Calvary's cross. "

—Oswald Chambers

Missing Out

Softball game's in progress, and the crowd cheers as a young, lanky girl with hair tied back scurries to the plate. CRACK! The ball connects with the bat; a line drive heads straight at the pitcher. The natural born athlete catches the ball, throwing the runner out at first base. High fives all around as they win the little league championship. High school, game on the line, she fires a screaming pitch striking the batter out. College scouts take notice as she wins her high school championship. Criminal Justice major, playing third base in Cactus County. An intelligent college student, still a skilled athlete with a canon arm.

"Bang, bang, bang" knocks me back to reality. "Fox, last two!" barks the guard at my door. Looking at the walls of my cage, pictures of my beautiful baby girl who has grown into a lovely young lady; the life I missed. What if I did not follow my older brother around the streets of Los Angeles, terrorizing our community? I would have been there to raise my daughter? What if I did not pull that gun from my waistband and take Frank's life? What if I did not choose the gang life over taking care of my baby girl, being the father she deserved? I would have been in Arizona, cheering her on while playing third.

Nicholas

" Trust in the LORD with all your heart And do not lean on your own understanding. In all your ways acknowledge Him, And He will make your paths straight. "

Proverbs 3:5-6

Everything Doesn't Stay the Same

My name is Eddie. Most likely we have never met, and probably never will. But if we do, I pray it's not under the circumstances that I'm currently in. I'm incarcerated and have been for seventeen years. I'm thirty-four years old now. For those of you who ditched school like I did, you might want to hear what I have to say. I was sixteen years old when I caught this case. I still have eight more years to do before the California Parole Board considers letting me out. I am the same age now that my single mother was when I came in. Imagine that for yourselves. She would always tell me, "Everything doesn't stay the same."

> **"**If I was a bully it was ok because it was a dog eat dog world and I was going to get you before you got me.**"**

Looking back, I understand too well the wisdom she tried to share with me. Back then though, I hardened my heart. I justified my anger towards her and everyone else. If I was a bully, it was ok, because it was a dog-eat-dog world, and I was going to get you before you got me. I used drugs, alcohol, violence and criminal behavior to mask my hurts. If my father didn't want anything to do with me, and if my family didn't live up to my standards of what a family should be, I found it in a gang. Not wanting or knowing how to deal with my issues in a positive way, I caused myself more problems by leaning on my own understanding. I was too busy looking at myself that I didn't take into consideration that my mom was trying her best to raise me with what she had. My mom didn't ask for my father to leave us while she was pregnant at sixteen. She truly believed that the best thing to do was to drop out of school and start working. She hoped that my sister's dad would be a good father, but he wasn't. Most of all, she never asked or wanted me to blame her for the mistakes I chose. But as any loving parent often does, she blamed herself.

As you are learning from your own lives, we deal with a lot of things. Some are tougher than others. While other people's problems seem easier than our own, take comfort in this: 1 Corinthians 10:13 "No temptation has overtaken you except what is common to mankind. And God is faithful; he will not let you be tempted beyond what you can bear. But when you are tempted, he will also provide a way out, so that you can endure it."

I am not going to lie to you. It was tough coming out of my comfort zone and asking for help from those that God placed around me. But, little by little, with His help, I began to see things differently. Understanding other people's situations, pain and hurts allowed me to be patient and compassionate towards people. Then soon, I started to take responsibility for my own choices. With the help of God, I stopped using drugs and alcohol to escape my problems. I worked hard to get what I needed or wanted, and it made me feel good about myself. You are going to have to decide for yourself if you really want the life you are headed down. Do you want it for your kids? I don't need to explain all the drama you're living in. You know it. But what I can do is share with you how it feels to be where you're at and trust in God with all your heart, mind and strength. I have a peace within me that I did not have on my own. While other guys crack under the pressures of not being with their loved ones, not having anyone, because they left them for whatever reasons, God has sustained me. He forgave me, so that I could forgive myself and those who have wronged me. Getting to know His love softened my heart to love myself and others. No longer did I need anyone's approval to make me feel good about myself. God has placed in me the courage to be who I am.

It has taken me a long time to find this peace. Don't take as long as I did. Decide today what you want, and place your trust in Christ.

Sincerely, Eddie

Falling to Freedom

My name is Chad. I'm thirty-seven years old, and I didn't grow up in a bad home. When I was young, I was always very impulsive, always eager to please. I was very outgoing, vibrant, and well...I always wanted to be a daredevil. When I was growing up, most people wanted to be a fireman. I wanted to be a stunt man.

> **"***I would say my life was basically a roller coaster. Extreme ups and extreme downs.***"**

At thirteen years old, I got arrested for my first grand theft auto. It wasn't like I was a big-time car thief or anything like that. I mean, basically, I just didn't want to walk. Now, I was in Juvenile Hall, and I felt hopeless. At that point, I knew that what I was doing wasn't right. From thirteen to fifteen years old, I was doing drugs. I would get off them, then back on them. I would say my life was basically a roller coaster. Extreme ups and extreme downs. I started doing methamphetamine at fifteen, then speed. Then I started using needles and shooting speed, and it wasn't long before I was arrested again, at fifteen, for another grand theft auto.

They gave me the opportunity to go to a drug treatment place that was like a therapeutic community, called the Phoenix House. For two years, I stayed there. I was clean; I did good. My junior year, I went to Santa Ana High School. I got straight A's, wrestled on the varsity wrestling team—everything seemed like it was turning around. It was great. Then, eventually, I started gravitating back to that old stuff. It wasn't long until I was doing speed and shooting speed again. At this time, I'm seventeen years old, and I basically bailed from my folks' house, and I'm living on the street, living in motels, living from house to house, and I got to a point where I realized, again, "What am I doing? This is crazy! I'm destroying my life again." I thought, maybe if I change my environment. So, I joined the Navy. I did good for a while, but eventually I gave a dirty drug test. They didn't kick me out right away, which was merciful. But I didn't quit using either. I gave another dirty test, four or five months later, and then they kicked me out of the Navy.

> *It's amazing where sin will take you and how hard your heart can become when you start to live a life of sin.*

Then something happened. I was supposed to go do a cook to make some drugs for a guy, and the deal basically went bad. Without going into details, I ended up getting in a fight with him. Later on, with my twisted thinking, I started imagining that this guy burned me at my opportunity to come up and make a little bit of money, so I went to rob him. I lacked feeling and compassion. When I went out to rob this guy, he basically told me that he didn't have any drugs, and I didn't believe him, so I shot him in the leg with a 9mm. I didn't even think about it. My life was so hard that I just did it. Then, in my twisted thinking, I started imaging this guy coming after me later, and I felt like I had no choice but to kill him. So that's what I did.

You know, it's amazing where sin will take you and how hard your heart can become when you start to live a life of sin. The things that might have bothered you before, no longer bother you. A lot of people that might use drugs, but not needles, think, "Well, I'd never do that. I smoke a little bud and I drink, but I'd never do that." Well, you know what, I thought the same thing. That's the way sin works. The things you could never see yourself doing at one point, if you continue in sin, all of a sudden they become possible.

The police and sheriff were doing their investigation, and one thing led to another, and I was found guilty of voluntary manslaughter at twenty-one years old. They gave me the max, which was eleven years. They gave me midterm on the burglary, which was four years. And they gave me four years for the use of a firearm, but I had to agree to take two strikes on this one case, which means if I were to pick up my third strike, I would be doing twenty-five-to-life. I remember saying, "God, if you'll get me out of this, then I'll serve you for the rest of my life." Maybe you've done that, or you're going to do that, but that doesn't work. After I was sentenced, I totally turned my back on God. Any supposed deal that I made with him was gone. I went headlong in to using the drugs again. In prison, I got involved in politics and the whole racial thing.

One day, a guy came by and he borrowed my outfit. That same day, the next unlock, the cop came and he hit my cell and he went through everything that was in my cell, and where I normally have that outfit, and my hypodermic needle was all tore apart. I realized at that point, had that cop found the needle, that would have been my third strike, and I would be doing twenty-five-to-life in prison. I knew at that moment something in my life had to change, or I was going to spend the rest of my life in prison.

> **"This guy now not only quit using drugs, but I saw him become a different person."**

That's when I ran into this guy that I used to do drugs with—a guy that was a scandalous dope fiend, the kind of dope fiend that would steal his grandma's medication money to go get a balloon, even though it may kill her, and he's going to go take it just to get some drugs. This guy, now, not only quit using drugs, but I saw him become a different person. The only thing I knew is that he started going to church. So, in my mind, I thought, well, if church can do it for him, then maybe it can do it for me. You know there's a saying that says, "No matter where you go, there you are." That's why I look at my life, and no matter what place I put myself or where I went, the problem was always there, because I was the problem. As I started going to church, my faith started building. In Romans 10:17 it says, "Faith comes by hearing and hearing by the Word of God." As I started hearing through the Word of God, whether through messages, or as I started to read the Bible, that faith started to build within my heart. In my brokenness, I surrendered my life to Christ. I never did the altar call. I never did any of that. But I would go through times where, because I lacked the faith for so long, it would be like one minute I knew God existed. I didn't have any physical proof. I didn't see the Red Sea part or anything like that. It was just that I knew in my heart that this is real. Then, the next minute, as quick as you could flip a light switch, I was thinking, This is a sham, I'm brainwashing myself, I'm making myself believe a lie, just so that I can get off drugs, and it was like this battle within my heart going back and forth.

> **"**I remember crying out to God and asking Him to give me the faith to be more involved, for Him to give me the faith to not be on the fence.**"**

I remember crying out to God and asking Him to give me the faith to be more involved, for Him to give me the faith to not be on the fence, and it was like the Lord spoke to me—not audibly, He just put it on my heart—"Chad, you have it backwards, if you get more involved, then I'll give you that faith. I won't give you the faith to get involved. You take that step of faith to get involved, you start reading your Word more, you start fellowshipping more, you start putting your heart into that, and then I'll give you the faith." You know what, eventually it got to the point where I said, "I know what the world has to offer, and I'm going the opposite way." At that point, I made a commitment to be in God's Word an hour a day. Now, that might not seem like a lot to some people, and maybe it seems like a whole lot to other people; but it wasn't long, maybe six months or something like that,

that I didn't doubt at all anymore. My faith had grown, and I got stronger. I didn't doubt God anymore.

Now comes in the grace, where God just starts blessing me with opportunities, things, people and resources, beyond anything I ever deserved. It all started with just opportunities within the church. Throughout time, the Lord gave me favor, and I was raised up to be a deacon in the church, and then eventually an elder in the church. Basically, I was pastoring in the church. I would do counseling and teaching. I taught books of the Bible, weekly studies and then services on Sunday.

One of the people God used, especially in the beginning, and has continued to use throughout my life, is a brother named Vernon, who at the time was serving life without parole. Vernon is now running Fully Embraced Ministries with me on the outside. God's Word says "What is impossible with man, is possible with God." Vern's life is a whole other testimony in itself.

My first four and a half years in prison were ones of wicked-ness and hopelessness, despair and destruction, where I was using and doing politics. But then, after I received the Lord, my last nine years in prison were ones of grace, mercy, steps of faith and God just dealing with that stuff that was in my heart. He was changing my mind, changing the way I thought about people, about my family, about His law, about His Word, about what's right and what's wrong.

By the time I paroled in January 2009, I had completed fifty units of an eighty-unit program at Calvary Chapel Bible College. The Lord had put it on my heart a while before that to not finish the classes while I was in there, but to leave some of the classes so that when I got out, I could actually come to the Bible College and take classes on campus. So that's what I did. I came and asked permission if I could take classes. Because of my background, they said yes, but I couldn't live on campus. For the first semester, I think I took ten units. I was trying to find a job, really couldn't find a job.

It was a little discouraging. Man, I am so thankful that God didn't give me favor before with any of those other jobs, because today I work full-time for Calvary Chapel Conference Center in Murrieta. I'm a welding fabricator; in fact, I run the welding shop now. I've been given extreme favor from the staff and from the leadership. I graduated the Bible College, December 2010.

> "We serve a gracious and merciful God and that He's ready and willing to forgive us for anything that we've done if we'll just humble ourselves and repent and submit our lives to Him."

Now, I actually teach for the Bible College. I am also now a pastor through Calvary Chapel Costa Mesa. I lead a ministry house called Fully Restored and Fully Embraced Ministries. We mentor men who are struggling with addictions, as well as open our home to men who are just getting out of prison and need help getting settled back on the outside. I mean, if that isn't grace, I don't know what is. Here I am a dirt bag, dope fiend, ex-con, and all I wanted to do was be able to come and take some classes at the Bible college. Now, I have a job that I love, being able to invest in the grounds here, and I get to teach for the Calvary Chapel Bible College. What a huge blessing.

One of the main reasons I tell my testimony is really to show that we serve a gracious and merciful God, and that he's ready and willing to forgive us for anything that we've done, if we'll just humble ourselves and repent and submit our lives to him. The other reason is that I know that there is deliverance only in the name of Jesus. He's delivered me from many things, specifically drug use. I just want to be able to encourage people that deliverance, salvation, doesn't come from a program, it doesn't come from a step, it doesn't come from a philosophy, but it comes from a person, and that person is Jesus Christ.

Sincerely, Chad

Closing

hope you have enjoyed these testimonies. I've been told many times that if it weren't for Jesus, many of these men would not be here today, they would probably be dead. But instead, they are redeemed and wanting to give back to society by sharing their stories with others in hopes that they might learn from their mistakes. I pray their words would be taken to heart and any who don't know Jesus would seek Him while He still may be found.

If you have never made a decision for Christ, you can right now. God's Word says "Today is the day of salvation." In Jeremiah 29:11 it also says that He has a plan for your life, a plan to prosper you and not to harm you, a plan to give you a hope and a future. In 2 Peter 3:9 it says He is not an angry God, He is patient with you, not wanting anyone to perish, but everyone to come to repentance.

His Word also says you must be born again. The only way to do that is through His Son Jesus Christ. Jesus says "I am the way, the truth and the life, no one can come to my Father but through me." John 14:6

So if you would like to be born again today and receive Jesus as your Lord and Savior, please pray this prayer:

Dear Lord Jesus,

I know I am a sinner. I believe You died for my sins and rose again on the third day according to the scriptures. I want to repent of my sins and ask for your forgiveness. I confess You as my personal Lord and Savior and thank You for making me a new creation, born again into the family of God.

In Jesus name, Amen

If you just said this prayer, welcome to God's family! Your name has just been written in the Lambs Book of Life. Salvation is a gift, it cannot be earned, only freely given. Jesus has guaranteed all who confess with their mouth that Jesus is Lord and believe in their heart that they will be saved. Now you get to experience His grace on a personal level! Now that you're saved, His Word says you were created for good works, and I can think of no better way to start your journey than to share with someone about your decision to follow Him. You can tell your cell mate, a friend, a relative, or write us and let us know. Also we'd love to hear what these testimonies have meant to you.

Our address is:

Pastors to Prisoners
P.O. Box 2757
La Mesa, CA 91943-2757

We encourage you to find a Bible believing group to study the Word of God with. Ask about being baptized as an outward act of obedience, showing others that you are now living a new life in Christ. Be prepared for God to write a new amazing chapter in your life, one full of grace, mercy and redemption! God bless you in your new exciting journey!

Dr. Roger Ziegler, Yard Pastor RJDCF

In this book you hear a lot about Pastor Roger Ziegler. After serving at RJ Donovan as a volunteer in the Protestant religious program for over 16 years, Roger has felt God's call to full-time ministry with Pastors to Prisoners as a Yard Pastor.

Roger is uniquely qualified for prison ministry. He has served in the KAIROS ministry; he has a Brown Card identification (which allows him to escort other volunteers); He teaches bible studies on several yards, and participated in chapel programs at other prisons such as Centinela, Soledad, Tehachapi, and Chowchilla as well as prisons in Arizona and Florida. He has also been a leader in ministries at his home church, and has shared his vision of ministering the Gospel of Jesus Christ to men who have lost all hope.

Roger has seen the fruit of his ministry in men who are now out of prison, and have found in their faith, the resources to experience not only a new life in Christ, but the power to experience the changes that allow for a new life of freedom and lawful productivity in the community.

Pastors to Prisoners Mission Statement

Pastors to Prisoners is a California non-profit organization providing ongoing financial support to ordained or licensed ministers uniquely burdened and willing to work with the incarcerated as full-time volunteer yard pastors under the direction of state chaplains in prison facilities. The goal for inmates is spiritual freedom in prison and success in society.

Roger gave up his chiropractic practice to follow what he believes in his heart to be God's call. He serves full-time at R. J. Donovan with his wife, Peggy (aka "Mamma Peggy"). They eagerly seek your prayers and support as Roger enters the "devil's playground" as a missionary of the Lord Jesus Christ. If you would like more information or would like to contact him, you can go to the pastorstoprisoners.org web site.

About the Author(s)

The authors of this book are the amazing men who shared their testimonies in hopes of helping others. I simply collected them and put them together in book form.

My name is Jenn. I was impacted by incarceration after my husband of 17 years was sentenced to 75 years behind bars without parole. In one year I went from being a married stay at home mom to being a divorced self-supporting single mother and completely at the mercy of God. It rocked my world to my very core. During the criminal hearings, I went on an extended fast seeking what the Lord would have me do with this brokenness that now consumed my heart. I begged Him to show me how He could use what the enemy intended for harm, for His glory. That's when the Lord showed up in a supernatural way.

The Lord opened my eyes and called me to serve those behind bars and bring the good news of the Gospel to all who would listen. He called me to show them the love of Jesus Christ. Little did I know that the very people I was once intimidated by would bring healing to my own heart through their love and encouragement. My compassion for those behind bars continues to grow and I can't think of a better place to share about a loving God then with those who feel they've been forgotten or misunderstood. He who has been forgiven much, loves much, and this is exactly what's taking place behind the walls. The privilege of putting this book together is the answer to my prayer so long ago. God does work all things together for the good of those that love Him and I pray that the testimonies in this book will touch your heart as they've touched mine!

Our stories, God's glory!